PHP 5

MIKE McGRATH

BARNES
&NOBLE
BOOKS
NEW YORK

In easy steps is an imprint of Computer Step
Southfield Road . Southam
Warwickshire CV47 0FB . United Kingdom
www.ineasysteps.com

This edition published for Barnes & Noble Books, New York
FOR SALE IN THE USA ONLY
www.bn.com

Notice of Liability
Every effort has been made to ensure that this book contains accurate
and current information. However, Computer Step and the author
shall not be liable for any loss or damage suffered by readers as a
result of any information contained herein.

Trademarks
All trademarks are acknowledged as belonging to their respective
companies.

Printed and bound in the United Kingdom

ISBN 0-7607-6331-3

Contents

Introducing PHP

Welcome to the exciting world of PHP server-side scripting. This chapter introduces PHP, describes how it works, then demonstrates how to establish a working development environment for PHP on the Windows operating system.

Covers

Chapter One

PHP in this book

This book is an introduction to the PHP 5 server-side scripting language using examples to demonstrate many different features.

PHP can be used to create interactive dynamic websites and is rapidly gaining in popularity because it is a flexible, cross-platform technology that provides amazingly powerful features.

You may have visited some impressive websites where the URL address ends with a file extension of ".php" or ".phtml". These are dynamic web pages served up to the web browser using the power of the PHP scripting language on the server.

The examples given throughout this book detail PHP source code and the resultant output that appears in the web browser.

What you need to know

PHP code exists alongside HTML code in the original PHP document on the server, so it is expected that you are familiar with the HyperText Markup Language (HTML).

Examples relating to databases use commands from the Structured Query Language (SQL). Previous knowledge of SQL is helpful, but not essential, as this book includes an introduction to basic SQL commands in a chapter introducing MySQL relational databases.

Code that is executed on the server, such as PHP, is called "server-side" code whereas code that is executed by the browser, such as JavaScript, is "client-side" code.

Those readers with some experience of other scripting languages, such as JavaScript, will more quickly understand some of the examples, but no previous knowledge of scripting is assumed by the book's text – you don't need to be a JavaScript guru to learn PHP!

Required software

The book provides instructions on how to create a PHP development environment under the Windows operating system combining the free Apache web server, the free MySQL database server and the free PHP processor itself. This allows you to test PHP scripts on your own personal computer before launching them live on the global Internet, or on a local intranet.

What is PHP?

"PHP" is a recursive acronym for "PHP: Hypertext Preprocessor". It has evolved from the "Personal Home Page" tools created in 1994 by independent I.T. contractor, Rasmus Lerdorf, to track users accessing his website. As these provoked much interest, he developed PHP into a scripting engine with a "Form Interpreter", released in 1996 as "PHP-FI".

Developers around the world began contributing ideas and by 1997 over 50,000 websites were using PHP-FI. Two of these developers, Zeev Suraski and Andi Gutmans, were primarily responsible for creating an Application Programming Interface (API) that became the PHP parser released in 1998 as "PHP 3".

Discover more about the Zend engine online at www.zend.com.

In 1999 the updated version of "PHP 4" incorporated the "Zend" engine (Zeev and Andi) so that PHP scripting could be used with any combination of web server, operating system and platform.

The latest version, "PHP 5", incorporates better security features and adds support for XML and object-oriented programming.

PHP is now used in over 16 million domains worldwide and its popularity continues to grow. Its stated goal is "to allow web developers to write dynamically generated pages quickly". With PHP you can read and write files, gather and process form data, send data via email, access and manipulate database records, read and write cookies, maintain data in session variables, facilitate user authentication, and much more.

Advantages of PHP

In addition to the cross-platform abilities mentioned above, PHP offers speed of execution using only meagre system resources, so it will not slow down the host machine. It uses its own resource management system, and has a sophisticated method for handling variables, thereby ensuring stability. Its simplicity allows anyone with a basic knowledge of HTML to start integrating PHP into their web pages straight away.

PHP's modular system of extensions allows it to interface with different libraries, such as encryption, graphics or XML, and adding further extensions is very simple.

How does PHP work?

A typical PHP document will contain one or more PHP elements, HTML markup elements, and the actual textual page content.

When a web browser requests a PHP page from a web server that is PHP-enabled, the server will call up the PHP parser to process all the PHP elements on that page.

The PHP parser executes the PHP script instructions on the page, generating a HTML document that is then sent to the web browser as a response to the original request.

The PHP parser may also be asked to retrieve information from a database, so the entire process appears like the illustration below:

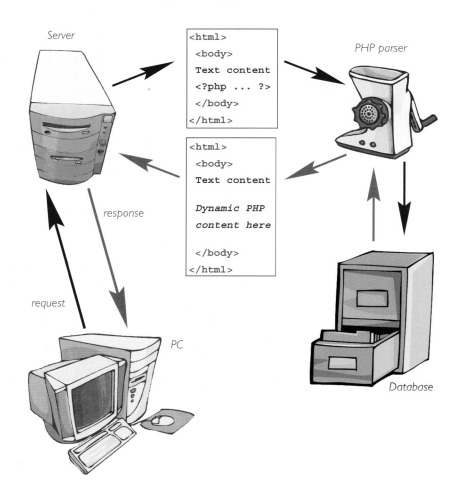

Creating a PHP environment

Typically, in order to develop and run PHP web pages, these three vital components need to be installed on the computer system:

Apache

MySQL

- **Web server** - PHP will work with virtually all web server software, including Microsoft's Internet Information Server (IIS), but is most often used with the freely available Apache server. All examples in this book are run on Apache 1.3.31.

- **Database** - PHP will work with virtually all database software, including Oracle and Sybase, but is most often used with the free MySQL database software for which it has specific optimizations. The popularity of MySQL is justified by its speed and scalability, which makes it suitable for deployment on high-traffic websites. All database examples in this book are shown using MySQL 4.0.18.

- **PHP parser** - In order to process PHP script instructions, a parser must be installed to generate HTML output that can be sent to the web browser. The parser engine is identical, irrespective of the operating system, so PHP pages need no changes to run on different platforms. All examples in this book use the parser in the final release of PHP 5.0.0.

As the Windows platform is by far the most popular desktop operating system it is convenient to establish a PHP environment in Windows to develop and test PHP scripts. Completed scripts may then be deployed on a Windows server or be uploaded to a web server running a different operating system.

In fact, most web servers run on the free Linux platform, which provides the reliability needed for minimum downtime and has robust security. The acronym "LAMP" is often used to describe their typical configuration of Linux, Apache, MySQL and PHP.

The rest of this chapter demonstrates how to download and install each of the three components needed to establish a PHP development environment on a Windows platform.

Installing Apache

Apache is the world's most popular web server, which, according to a recent survey, accounts for 56% of all web servers worldwide. It can be freely downloaded from http://httpd.apache.org or one of the mirrors listed on that site.

Download the stable version for Windows – this will be named something like "apache_1.3.31-win32-x86-no_src.msi". Double-click on the downloaded file to begin installation, then complete the input fields in the Server Information dialog box like this:

 Ensure that you name the server "localhost" and that the radio button to "Run as a service for All Users" is selected.

PHP 5.0.0 Final release regards Apache2 as experimental. It recommends that you use Apache 1.3.x instead.

 Installing at C:\ automatically creates an Apache directory as C:\Apache.

When the Setup Type dialog box appears, choose the option to have a "complete" installation. Finally, in the Destination Folder dialog box, change the suggested installation location to just C:\, then complete the installation. The Apache web server should now be running in the background. To verify this, open a web browser and type "http://localhost" (without the quotes) in the address field and then hit Enter to display the default Apache page.

Starting & stopping Apache

If Apache has been installed with the recommended option to "Run as a service for All Users" it will constantly run in the background and so be available via "http://localhost" at any time.

Alternatively, if Apache has been installed with the option to "Run when started manually", it can be started from the command line by typing "NET START apache" at a prompt. Similarly it can be stopped by typing "NET STOP apache". In each case a status comment is reported in the command window, as seen below:

Either of these techniques can also be used to start and stop the MySQL server.

An alternative means of controlling background services is available on Windows XP. All services can be displayed by navigating through Start > Control Panel > Administrative Tools > Services. Click on the "Apache" service in the list then select the option to "Stop" or "Restart" the service. When Apache is stopped, an option to "Start" the service lets you start Apache running again.

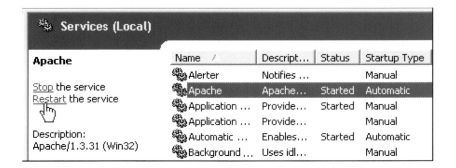

Installing MySQL

There are a various database servers available for purchase, such as Microsoft Access, but the MySQL database server is both powerful and free. It is in widespread use on web servers running PHP and can be freely downloaded from www.mysql.com.

Download the binary release version of MySQL for Windows, named for example "mysql-4.0.18-win.zip". Unzip this file then double-click on the extracted file called "setup.exe" to start the installation. During setup accept the suggested installation location of C:\mysql and opt for a "Typical" installation. The MySQL user manual can be found later in the "Docs" subdirectory.

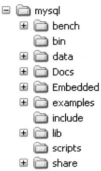

Before starting the MySQL database server, you must place a configuration file in your system's root directory – templates are provided for this purpose. Typically you should copy the template file at C:\mysql\my-medium.cnf to C:\ and rename it as "my.cnf". The options set in this file are read when the MySQL service starts.

The C:\mysql\bin folder contains all the executable files needed to run MySQL. On Windows XP, 2000 and NT systems, MySQL can be installed as a service that runs in the background, other platforms have to run MySQL manually as an application.

Type "C:\mysql\bin\mysqld-nt --install" at a command prompt to install MySQL as a background service that will automatically start whenever your computer gets started. It can be started manually from a prompt with the command "NET START mysql" and be stopped with the command "NET STOP mysql". With MySQL running type "C:\mysql\bin\mysql" to launch the MySQL monitor where databases can be created and manipulated:

The MySQL monitor can be closed to return to a regular prompt by typing "quit" or "exit" at the mysql> prompt.

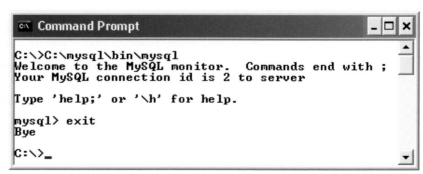

Installing PHP

The final component needed to establish a PHP development environment is PHP itself. This can be freely downloaded from www.php.net. The version for Windows will be named like "php-5.0.0-Win32.zip". Download this archive, then extract its contents to a convenient location, such as C:\php.

The extracted files include one named "php.ini-recommended", which is a template PHP configuration file. Copy this file to your C:\Windows folder then rename it as "php.ini".

The "php.ini" is simply a text file that can be opened in any text editor, such as Windows Notepad application. With Apache installed at C:\Apache and PHP installed at C:\php (as described in this chapter) ensure that the "php.ini" configuration file correctly identifies the root Apache directory and the PHP extensions directory by finding these two lines:

```
doc_root = "C:\Apache\htdocs"

extension_dir = "C:\php\ext"
```

If PHP installation has not automatically created these they can be edited manually to read as above – remember to then save the file.

MySQL support is present in PHP 5, but may not be enabled by default. To enable it manually, first open "php.ini" once more then find the following line:

```
extension = "php_mysql.dll"
```

If necessary, remove the semi-colon at the start of this line so it is no longer "commented out", then save the file. Now copy the MySQL library file at C:\php\libmysql.dll and paste it into your C:\Windows\System folder.

This completes the PHP installation, but before it can be tested with a browser, modifications need to be made to the Apache configuration so that it can recognize PHP examples and know how to handle them. The rest of this chapter describes how to modify the Apache configuration and how to test the PHP environment.

Configuring Apache for PHP

Before the Apache server can run PHP examples it must be told where to find the PHP module and how to recognize PHP files. This is achieved by editing the Apache configuration file located at C:\Apache\conf\httpd.conf.

Open the "httpd.conf" configuration file in a text editor, then find the section containing the "AddModule" directives. At the end of that section add the following three lines:

```
LoadModule php5_module c:/php/php5apache.dll

AddModule mod_php5.c

AddType application/x-httpd-php .php .phtml
```

The first two lines identify the PHP module. The final line defines a MIME type for files ending with a file extension of ".php" and ".phtml" so they will be processed by the PHP parser on request.

Save the file to include these newly added configuration directives.

"MIME" is an acronym for "Multipurpose Internet Mail Extensions" – which is a standard for defining file type formats.

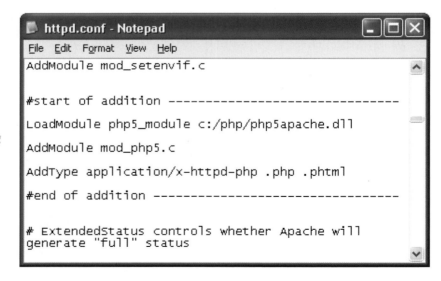

Rebooting your system now will ensure that the MySQL, PHP and Apache services get started with all the configuration changes applied and ready to be tested.

Testing PHP

phpinfo.php

To create an initial PHP file that can be used to test the environment, open a text editor and type this line of code:

```
<?php phpinfo(); ?>
```

Save the file as "phpinfo.php" and place it in Apache's "htdocs" folder. This location is where Apache automatically looks for files that have been requested by a web browser.

Now, with Apache running, open a web browser and type into its URL address field "http://localhost/phpinfo.php". Hit the Enter key and PHP will generate a web page, similar to the one below, listing important information about your PHP environment.

Testing MySQL connection

As a final test of the development environment a PHP script can be executed (via the Apache web server) to ensure that a connection can be made to the MySQL server running on your system. This will involve all three components of the environment.

The test script is listed below within the HTML "body" section of a document. It is explained in more detail later but, for now, it can be simply copied verbatim to check the MySQL connection. Use the Notepad text editor to write the file, then save it as "mysqltest.php" in Apache's "htdocs" folder.

mysqltest.php

```
<html>
<head> <title>MySQL Connection Test</title> </head>
<body>
<h2>

<?php
  $connection = mysql_connect( "localhost", "root", "" )
   or die( "Sorry - unable to connect to MySQL" );
   echo( "Congratulations - you connected to MySQL" );
?>

</h2>
</body> </html>
```

When "http://localhost/mysqltest.php" is requested in a browser address field, the PHP parser executes the script code, and a message will appear in the generated HTML stating the test result. If the test succeeds the generated output looks like this screenshot:

Getting started with PHP

All the examples that follow in this book are identical on both Windows and Linux platforms except that, where paths are mentioned, they should be appropriate to the operating system. For instance, the typical Apache root directory in Windows is at C:\Apache\htdocs and in Linux it's at /usr/local/apache/htdocs.

This chapter introduces the PHP syntax requirements and demonstrates how to use variables and functions.

Covers

Chapter Two

Hello World

All PHP code must be included inside special markup tags that are recognized by the PHP parser. Each PHP code tag begins with "<?php" and ends with "?>", and looks like this:

```
<?php    PHP code goes here    ?>
```

In older PHP scripts the code was sometimes written inside a tag that just began "<?", rather than "<?php". This is discouraged in PHP 5 to avoid confusion with other server-side languages, so the "<?php" version is used throughout this book. Whenever a tag beginning with "<?php" is encountered, its contents are automatically referred to the PHP parser for interpretation.

Because the echo() function is so frequently used, the PHP parser allows its parentheses to be optionally omitted.

The most basic PHP instruction is the echo() function, which is used to make the PHP parser dynamically write content into a generated HTML page. Literal content must be enclosed within quotes inside the function's parentheses and may include HTML markup tags. In the simple example below, the echo() function writes a traditional welcome message as a heading in a HTML page:

hello.php

```
<html>

<?php echo( "<h1>Hello World</h1>" ); ?>

</html>
```

This example is saved in Apache's "htdocs" folder so that it can be viewed in a web browser by typing "http://localhost/hello.php" in the browser URL field, like this:

All examples in this book will be saved in the htdocs folder and requested via Apache using http://localhost/ to address them – opening the file directly in a browser will not process the PHP code.

Syntax rules

PHP is not generally case-sensitive, so the example on the opposite page could have been written as follows and still produced the same result when viewed in a web browser:

Normally use only lowercase characters for all PHP code.

```
<html>

<?PHP ECHO( "<H1>Hello World</H1>" ); ?>

</html>
```

It is important to notice the semi-colon at the end of the PHP instruction. This terminator must appear at the end of each PHP statement, in the same way that a period must terminate each sentence in the English language.

Comments can usefully be added inside the PHP code block as explanation to third parties, or as a reminder when you revisit the code later. The PHP parser sees any text between "//" and the end of that line as a single-line comment, which it ignores. Alternatively, single-line comments may begin with a "#" character. Also, text on one or more lines between "/*" and "*/" is ignored.

comments.php

```
<html>

<?php

/* Here is an introduction to this script code inside
     a multi-line comment block */

 echo ( "<h1>Hello World</h1>" );

// Here is single-line comment

# And here is another single-line comment

?>

</html>
```

When this example is opened in a web browser, via Apache, the browser's View > Source menu option reveals only this code:

```
<html> <h1>Hello World</h1> </html>
```

Escaping characters

The "\" backslash character can be used to apply special significance to the character that immediately follows it. This is especially useful to include quotation marks within a string of text to be written with the echo() function. As the string is itself enclosed by quotes, the PHP parser would be confused by additional quotes and deliver an error message. This is easily avoided by preceding the additional quotes by a backslash character to escape them.

Single quotes or double quotes may be used to enclose strings.

Additionally the newline syntax "\n" can be used to move to a new line in text areas and "\t" to tab across a text area.

The following example creates a HTML text area containing text content that includes an escaped quotation and demonstrates the newline and tab features. The quotes containing the HTML attribute values for rows and columns (cols) are also escaped.

escape.php

```
<html>
<?php
echo( "<textarea rows=\"5\" cols=\"48\">" );
echo
  ( "\"Utinam populus Romanus unam cervicem haberet!\"" );
echo
  ( "\n(Would that the Roman people had but one neck!)" );
echo( "\n\n \t\t\t Caligula A.D. 12-41" );
echo( "</textarea>" );
?>
</html>
```

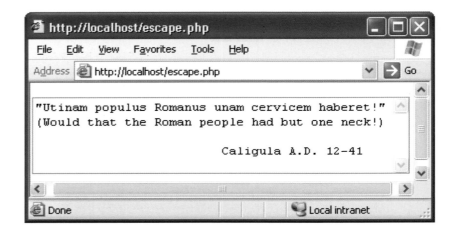

Reserved words

The table on this page contains words that are part of the PHP language itself. They may not be used when choosing identifier names for variables, functions or labels.

Keywords	eval()	switch
and	exception	TRUE
array()	exit()	unset()
as	extends	use
break	FALSE	var
case	for	xor
cfunction	foreach	while
class	function	
const	global	**Constants**
continue	if	_FILE_
declare	include()	_LINE_
default	include_once()	_FUNCTION_
do	isset()	_CLASS_
die()	list()	_METHOD_
echo()	new	
else	NULL	**Predefined Variables**
elseif	old_function	
empty()	or	_COOKIE
enddeclare	php_user_filter	_ENV
endfor	print()	_GET
endforeach	require()	_POST
endif	require_once()	_REQUEST
endswitch	return()	_SERVER
endwhile	static	_SESSION

Variables

A variable is a place in which to store data for manipulation within a PHP script. All variables begin with a "$" character, followed by a meaningful name of your choice. When naming variables, any letters, digits and the "_" underscore character may be used, but the variable name may not begin with a digit. These are all valid variable names:

```
$abc

$my_first_variable

$var123
```

Variable names are case-sensitive – so $var and $VAR are treated as separate, individual variables.

Data is assigned to a variable using the "=" operator. The assignation statement, like all PHP statements, should end with a semi-colon terminator.

The example below recreates the text area example from page 22. In this case though, the entire text content is assigned to a variable called $str. This makes the script more efficient because the whole text content is now written into the text area with just a single call to the echo() function, rather than the five calls used previously.

firstvar.php

```
<html>
<?php

$str = "<textarea rows=\"5\" cols=\"48\">\"Utinam
populus Romanus unam cervicem haberet!\"\n(Would that
the Roman people had but one neck!)\n\n \t\t\t Caligula
A.D. 12-41</textarea>";

echo( $str );
?>
</html>
```

Notice that the $str variable is not surrounded by quotes in the call to the echo() function because it is not to be treated literally.

Opening this example in a web browser, via Apache, produces precisely the same generated page as that of the previous example shown at the bottom of page 22.

Data types

PHP is a loosely typed language, so its variables can store different types of data, such as numbers, text strings or boolean values. This is unlike many programming languages, such as C++ and Java, that must declare a variable to be of a specific data type and may then store only data of the declared type inside that variable.

Data types that can be stored in PHP variables include:

- String – strings of spaces, text and numeric characters specified within double quotes ("...") or single quotes ('...')

- Integer – numbers without decimal places, such as 1,000

- Floating-point – numbers with decimal places, like 3.142

- Boolean – a truth value expressed with the case-insensitive PHP keywords of TRUE or FALSE.

When assigning numeric values to a variable they should not be enclosed in quotes else they will be treated as string values.

Additionally a variable can be set to have no value at all by assigning it the case-insensitive PHP keyword of NULL.

vartype.php

```
<html>
<?php        $str = "Here is a string";
             $int = 77; $flt = 3.142; $non = NULL;
             echo( "String:$str<br>" );
             echo( "Integer:$int<br>" );
             echo( "Floating-point:$flt<br>" );
             echo( "Null:$non" );
?>
</html>
```

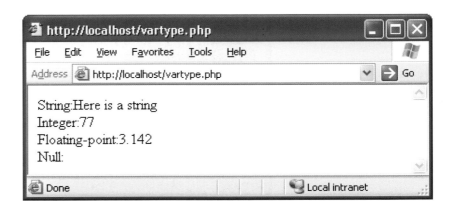

Functions

A function is a piece of PHP code that can be executed once or many times by the PHP script. Functions and variables form the basis of all PHP scripts.

PHP has lots of intrinsic functions, such as echo(), but you can create your own using the "function" keyword in a declaration. This is followed by a space, then a chosen name for your function (following the same naming conventions used when naming variables). The function name is always followed by a pair of plain brackets, then a pair of curly brackets containing the actual code that is to be executed whenever that function is called.

In this example the function has been named go() and it will write a short message and horizontal ruled line whenever it is called.

firstfcn.php

This example uses separate PHP elements to declare and call a function.

```php
<html> <head> <title>PHP Functions</title> </head>
<body>
<?php function go()
        { echo( "PHP adds dynamic content<hr>" ); } ?>

<?php go(); ?>

<p>*** HTML is great for static content ***</p>

<?php go(); ?>

</body> </html>
```

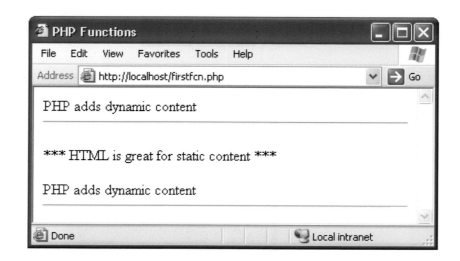

Function arguments

The plain brackets that follow all function names can be used to provide data for use in the code to be executed by that function, just as the brackets of the PHP echo() function contain the string that is to be written in the generated page.

The data contained within the brackets is known as the function "argument". In the following example, the function call passes string values to the go() function's $arg argument for use in the code that is to be executed. In this case the string value passed from the function call is written out in bold, underlined italic text.

arg.php

```
<html>
<head> <title>PHP Arguments</title> </head>
<body>

<?php function go( $arg )
    { echo( "<b><u><i>$arg</i></u></b>" ); } ?>

<p>This is the regular text style of this page.</p>

<?php go( "This text has added style" ); ?>

<p>This is the regular text style of this page.</p>

<?php go( "PHP makes this so easy" ); ?>

</body> </html>
```

Numeric argument values can be passed for manipulation by the function code.

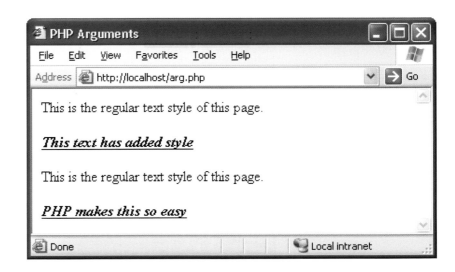

Multiple functions

PHP functions may call other functions during the execution of their code in just the same way that the previous examples called the echo() function.

The following example demonstrates the use of multiple functions to manipulate and display an integer argument value.

functions.php

```php
<?php
    function show_number( $num )
    {
      $new_number = make_double( $num );
      echo( "The value is $new_number" );
    }

    function make_double( $arg )
    {
      return $arg + $arg;
    }
?>

<html> <head> <title>PHP Functions</title> </head>
<body>
    <h3> <?php show_number(4); ?> </h3>
</body>
</html>
```

Note the code format of this example – when defining functions, the source code is clearer if all declarations appear before any HTML or page content.

The argument value is passed from the calling statement to the make_double() function via the show_number() function. The passed argument value is doubled, then the result is returned to a variable in the show_number() function. Finally the echo() function is called to write the new value out on the page.

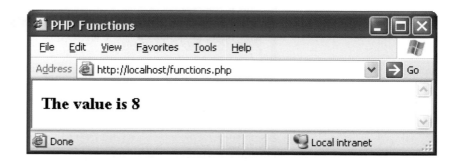

Variable scope

Variable scope defines which parts of a PHP script have access to a variable. The variables used in the example on the opposite page are both declared inside functions, so are known as "local" variables. These can be used by only the function in which they are declared.

Conversely, "global" variables are declared outside functions and can be accessed by any function in that document. Unlike other languages that make global variables accessible automatically, PHP requires a function to declare explicitly that it wants to use a global variable, otherwise the variable will be deemed to be of local scope by default. A simple declaration inside a function's code block uses the "global" keyword followed by the variable name.

This example creates a global variable $num, made accessible to two functions by including a declaration in each code block.

scope.php

```php
<?php $num;

    function make_triple( $arg )
    {
        global $num;
        $num = $arg + $arg +$arg;
        thrice();      }

    function thrice()
    {
        global $num;
        echo( "The value is $num" );        }
?>

<html> <head> <title>Variable Scope</title> </head>
<body> <h3> <?php make_triple(4); ?> </h3> </body></html>
```

Removal of either global declaration will render the code useless, as PHP then assumes the variable reference in the function is made to a local variable.

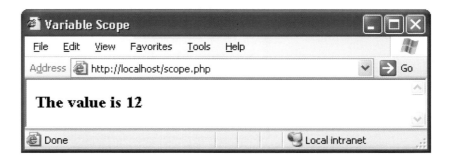

Multiple arguments

Functions may specify multiple arguments within their plain brackets to allow several values to be passed to the function code. The argument variable names simply need to be separated by commas in a list.

When a function specifies single or multiple arguments, all calls to that function must also normally include the correct number of argument values to avoid an error. Optionally, a default value can be assigned to the argument in the function declaration.

In this example, three arguments are specified, each with a default value to be used if no argument value is passed from the caller:

args.php

```php
<?php

    function addup( $a = 32, $b = 32, $c = 32 )
    {
      $total = $a + $b + $c;
      echo("$a + $b + $c = $total");
    }
?>

<html> <head> <title>Function Arguments</title> </head>
<body>

  <h3> <?php addup(8, 16, 24); ?> </h3>

  <h3> <?php addup(8, 16); ?> </h3>

</body> </html>
```

![Function Arguments browser window showing http://localhost/args.php]

8 + 16 + 24 = 48

8 + 16 + 32 = 56

Performing operations

This chapter introduces the different PHP operators and demonstrates how they can be used in script statements to perform comparisons and to manipulate values.

Covers

Chapter Three

Arithmetical operators

The arithmetical operators commonly used in PHP scripts are listed in the table below together with the operations they perform:

Operator	Operation
+	Numeric addition
.	String concatenation
-	Subtraction
*	Multiplication
/	Division
%	Modulus
++	Increment
- -	Decrement

Notice that the **+** operator cannot be used to join together strings as it can in other languages. It will add together two numeric values and give the result of the addition. Concatenation of strings can only be performed with the . dot operator.

The modulus operator will divide the first given number by the second given number and return the remainder of the operation. This is most useful to determine if a number is odd or even.

The increment **++** and decrement **--** operators alter the given value by 1 and return the resulting new value. These are most commonly used to count iterations in a loop.

All the other operators act as you would expect, but care should be taken to bracket expressions where more than one operator is being used, to clarify the operations:

An example using the modulus operator to determine odd or even values can be found in the "if statement" example on page 42.

```
a = b * c - d % e / f ;          \\ This is unclear

a = (b * c) - ((d % e) / f );    \\ This is clearer
```

arithmetical.php

```php
<?php
    $addnum = 20+30;
    $addstr = "I love " . "PHP";
    $sub = 35.75 - 28.25;
    $mul = 8 * 50;
    $mod = 65 % 2;
    $inc = 5; ++$inc;
    $dec = 5; --$dec;

    $result = "addnum:$addnum  <br>";
    $result .= "addstr:$addstr <br>";
    $result .= "sub:$sub        <br>";
    $result .= "mul:$mul        <br>";
    $result .= "mod:$mod        <br>";
    $result .= "inc:$inc        <br>";
    $result .= "dec:$dec        <br>";

?>

<html>
<head> <title>Arithmetical Operators</title> </head>
<body>
    <h3> <?php echo( $result ); ?> </h3>
</body>
</html>
```

The increment and decrement operators may also be used following the operand where they will perform the operation but return the original value.

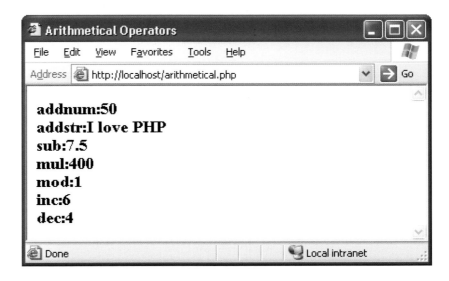

Logical operators

The table below lists the PHP logical operators:

Operator	Operation
&&	Logical AND
and	Logical AND
||	Logical OR
or	Logical OR
xor	Logical exclusive XOR
!	Logical NOT

The logical operators are used with operands that have the boolean values of true or false, or are values that can convert to true or false.

The logical "&&" and "and" operators will evaluate two operands and return true only if both operands themselves are true. Otherwise they will return false. This is typically used in conditional branching, where the direction of a script is determined by testing two conditions: If both conditions are satisfied the script will go in a certain direction, otherwise it will take a different direction.

The "||" and "or" operators will evaluate two operands and return true if either one of the operands itself returns true. If neither operand returns true they will return false. This is useful to perform an action if either one of two test conditions has been met.

The "xor" operator will evaluate its two operands and return true only if either one of the operands itself returns true but not both.

The "!" logical not is a unary operator that is used before a single operand. It returns the inverse value of the given operand – so if a variable "a" had a value of true then "!a" would have a value of false. This is useful in PHP scripts to toggle the value of a variable in successive loop iterations with a statement like a=!a. This will ensure that on each pass the value is changed, like flicking a light switch on and off.

logical.php

```php
<?php        $a = true; $b = false;

     #test both operands for true
     $test1 = ( $a and $a )? "true":"false";
     $test2 = ( $a and $b )? "true":"false";
     $test3 = ( $b and $b )? "true":"false";

     #test either operand for true
     $test4 = ( $a or $a )? "true":"false";
     $test5 = ( $a or $b )? "true":"false";
     $test6 = ( $b or $b )? "true":"false";

     #test for single operand is true
     $test7 = ( $a xor $a )? "true":"false";
     $test8 = ( $a xor $b )? "true":"false";
     $test9 = ( $b xor $b )? "true":"false";

     #invert values
     $test10 = ( !$a )? "true":"false";
     $test11 = ( !$b )? "true":"false";

     $result = "AND - 1:$test1 2:$test2 3:$test3<br>";
     $result .= "OR - 1:$test4 2:$test5 3:$test6<br>";
     $result .= "XOR - 1:$test7 2:$test8 3:$test9<br>";
     $result .= "NOT - 1:$test10 2:$test11";
?>

<html><head><title>Logical Operators</title></head>
<body>   <?php echo( $result ); ?> </body></html>
```

To display the results this example uses the conditional operator, which is described on page 40.

AND - 1:true 2:false 3:false
OR - 1:true 2:true 3:false
XOR - 1:false 2:true 3:false
NOT - 1:false 2:true

Assignment operators

The operators that are commonly used in PHP to assign values are all listed in the table below. Each of them except the simple = assign operator is a shorthand form of a longer expression, so each equivalent is also given for clarity.

Operator	Example	Equivalent
=	$a = $b	$a = $b
+= (for numbers)	$a += $b	$a = $a + $b
.= (for strings)	$a .= $b	$a = $a . $b
-=	$a -= $b	$a = $a - $b
*=	$a *= $b	$a = $a * $b
/=	$a /= $b	$a = $a / $b
%=	$a %= $b	$a = $a % $b

The equality operator compares values and is explained fully, with examples, on page 38.

It is important to regard the = operator as meaning "assign" rather than "equals" to avoid confusion with the == equality operator. In the example in the table, the variable named $a is assigned the value that is contained in the variable named $b, taking this as its new value.

In the table example, the += operator adds the numeric value contained in variable $a to the numeric value contained in the variable named $b and then assigns the result as the new value contained in variable $a.

The .= operator is very useful and has been used in earlier examples to add a second string to an existing string.

All the other operators in the table work in the same way as the += operator, by making the arithmetical operation between the two values first, then assigning the result to the first variable.

assignment.php

```php
<?php
    $a = "PHP "; $aa = "Script"; #assign string values
    $a .= $aa; #concatenate strings and assign to $a

    $b = 8; $bb = 4; #assign integer values
    $b += $bb; #add numbers and assign result to $b

    $c = 7.5; $cc = 2.25; #assign float values
    $c -= $cc; #subtract and assign result to $c

    $d = 8; $dd = 4; #assign integer values
    $d *= $dd; #multiply and assign result to $d

    $e = 8; $ee = 4; #assign integer values
    $e /= $ee; #divide and assign result to $e

    $f = 8; $ff = 4; #assign integer values
    $f %= $ff; #divide and assign remainder to $f

    $result =  "\$a ADD AND ASSIGN STRING: $a<br>";
    $result .= "\$b ADD AND ASSIGN INTEGER: $b<br>";
    $result .= "\$c SUBTRACT AND ASSIGN FLOAT: $c<br>";
    $result .= "\$d MULTIPLY AND ASSIGN: $d<br>";
    $result .= "\$e DIVIDE AND ASSIGN: $e<br>";
    $result .= "\$f MODULO AND ASSIGN: $f";
?>

<html><head><title>Assignment Operators</title></head>
<body> <?php echo( $result ); ?> </body></html>
```

Using the .= operator with numbers will concatenate them – so that 8 .= 4 gives 84, not 12.

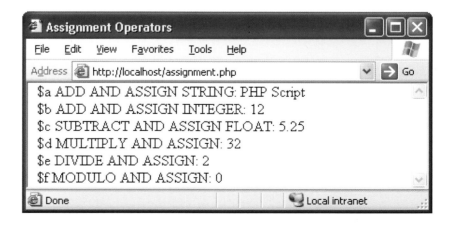

$a ADD AND ASSIGN STRING: PHP Script
$b ADD AND ASSIGN INTEGER: 12
$c SUBTRACT AND ASSIGN FLOAT: 5.25
$d MULTIPLY AND ASSIGN: 32
$e DIVIDE AND ASSIGN: 2
$f MODULO AND ASSIGN: 0

Comparison operators

The operators that are commonly used in PHP to compare two values are listed in the table below:

Operator	Comparative Test
==	Equality
!=	Inequality
>	Greater than
<	Less than
>=	Greater than or equal to
<=	Less than or equal to

The equality operator == compares two operands and returns true if both are equal in value: If both are the same number then they are equal, or if both are strings containing the same characters in the same positions then they are equal. Boolean operands that are both true, or both false, are equal.

Conversely the != inequality operator returns true if two operands are not equal, using the same rules as the == equality operator.

Equality and inequality operators are useful in testing the state of two variables to perform conditional branching.

The > greater than operator compares two operands and will return true if the first is greater in value than the second.

The < less than operator makes the same comparison, but returns true if the first operand is lesser in value than the second.

Adding the = operator after a > greater than or < less than operator makes them also return true if the two operands are exactly equal in value.

The > greater than operator is frequently used to test the value of a countdown value in a loop.

An example of the less than operator < in a loop statement can be found on page 45.

comparison.php

```php
<?php
    $a = ("PHP"=="PHP")? "true":"false";
    $b = ("PHP"=="PERL")?"true":"false";

    $c = (1.785==1.785)? "true":"false";
    $d = (5 != 5)? "true":"false";

    $e = (true == true)? "true":"false";
    $f = (false != false)? "true":"false";

    $g = (100<200)? "true":"false";
    $h = (100<100)? "true":"false";

    $i = (100<=100)? "true":"false";
    $j = ( -1 > 1 )? "true":"false";

    $result =  "TEST STRINGS \$a:$a  \$b:$b<br>";
    $result .= "TEST NUMBERS \$c:$c \$d:$d<br>";
    $result .= "TEST BOOLEANS \$e:$e \$f:$f<br>";
    $result .= "TEST LESS THAN \$g:$g \$h:$h<br>";
    $result .= "TEST LESS THAN OR EQUAL \$i:$i<br>";
    $result .= "TEST GREATER THAN \$j:$j";
?>

<html><head><title>Comparison Operators</title></head>
<body>
    <?php echo( $result ); ?>
</body></html>
```

To display the results this example uses the conditional operator, which is described on page 40.

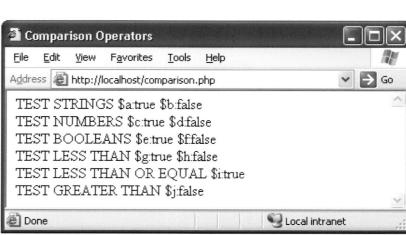

Conditional operator

The PHP coder's favorite operator is probably the conditional operator. This first evaluates an expression for a true or false value then executes one of two given statements depending upon the result of the evaluation. The conditional operator has this syntax:

```
( test-expression ) ? if-true-do-this : if-false-do-this ;
```

This operator can be used to assign an appropriate value to a variable, as seen in some examples earlier in this chapter, or to call a function, as demonstrated in the example below.

conditional.php

```php
<?php
    function is_odd()
    { global $num; echo( "$num is an odd number<hr>" ); }

    function is_even()
    { global $num; echo( "$num is an even number<hr>" );}
?>

<html><head><title>Conditional Operator</title></head>
<body>
<?php
    $num = 57;
    ( $num % 2 != 0 ) ? is_odd() : is_even();

    $num = 44;
    ( $num % 2 != 0 ) ? is_odd() : is_even();
?>
</body></html>
```

Notice that each function uses the "global" keyword to make the $num variable value accessible – see page 29 for details.

Making statements

Statements are used in PHP to progress the execution of the script. They may define loops within the code or be simple terms to be evaluated. This chapter introduces conditional testing and includes examples of different types of loops.

Covers

Chapter Four

Conditional if statement

The "if" keyword is used to perform the basic conditional PHP test to evaluate an expression for a boolean value. The statement following the evaluation will be executed only when the expression is true. The syntax for the "if" statement looks like this:

```
if ( test-expression ) statement-to-execute-when-true ;
```

The code to be executed may contain multiple statements if they are enclosed in a pair of curly brackets to form a "statement block".

In the example below the expression to be tested uses the modulus operator to determine if the value contained in the variable called $num is exactly divisible by 2. The statement block has two statements – one to assign a string value to a variable and another to call the PHP echo() function.

if.php

```php
<html>
    <head><title>If Statement</title></head>
<body>
<?php
    $num = 7;
    if ( $num % 2 != 0 )
    {
        $msg = "$num is an odd number.";
        echo( $msg );
    }
?>
</body></html>
```

This example could have used ($num%2!=1) to detect an even number.

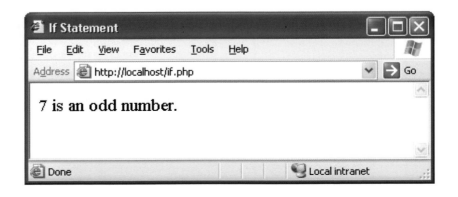

If–else statement

The PHP "else" keyword can be used with an "if" statement to provide alternative code to execute in the event that the tested expression is found to be false.

This is known as "conditional branching" and has this syntax:

```
if ( test-expression ) do-this ; else do-this ;
```

Several expressions may be tested until a true value is found, when the code following the true expression will be executed. It is important to note that any further code contained in the if-else statement is ignored.

In the following example, any code after the call to the echo() function by the successful third test will be ignored completely:

ifelse.php

```php
<html><head><title>If-else Statement</title></head>
<body>
<?php
 $num = 2;   $bool = false;

 if( $num==1 and $bool==true ) echo( "Test 1 success" );
 else
 if( $num==2 and $bool==true ) echo( "Test 2 success" );
 else
 if( $num==2 and $bool==false ) echo( "Test 3 success" );
 else
 if( $num==3 and $bool==false ) echo( "Test 4 success" );
?>
</body></html>
```

The semi-colon is required after the first code statement, before starting the "else" alternative code.

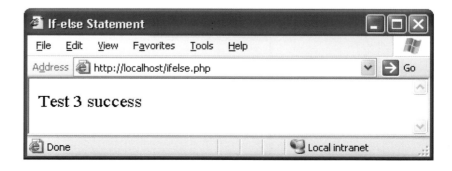

Switch statement

Conditional branching using an "if-else" statement can often be performed more efficiently using a "switch" statement, when the test expression evaluates the value of just one variable.

For more detail on the "break" statement see page 48.

The "switch" statement works in an unusual way. First it evaluates a given expression, then seeks a label to match the resulting value. The code associated with the matching label will be executed, or, if none of the labels match, the statement will execute any specified default code.

The PHP "case" keyword is used to denote a label, and the "default" keyword is used to specify the default code. All label code must be terminated by a break statement using the PHP "break" keyword.

The labels may be numbers, strings, or booleans, but must all be of the same type, like this example which uses numbers:

switch.php

```php
<html><head><title>Switch Statement</title></head>
<body>
<?php
      $num = 2;

      switch( $num )
      {
        case 1 : echo( "This is case 1 code" ); break;
        case 2 : echo( "This is case 2 code" ); break;
        case 3 : echo( "This is case 3 code" ); break;
        default : echo( "This is default code" );
      }
?>
</body></html>
```

Omission of the "break" keywords allows the execution of all other code in the switch statement.

For loop

The "for" loop is probably the most frequently used type of loop in PHP scripting, and has this syntax:

```
for( initializer , test , increment ) { statement/s }
```

The initializer is used to set the start value for the counter of the number of loop iterations. A variable may be declared here for this purpose, and it is traditional to name it $i.

On each pass of the loop an expression is tested for a boolean result and that iteration of the loop will run only if the result is true. The loop will end if the test result is false.

A "for" loop can count down by decrementing the counter on each iteration with $i--.

With every iteration the loop executes the code in the statement, then increments the counter within. Multiple statements can be executed if they are contained within curly brackets to form a statement block.

The following example makes five iterations and changes the assigned value of two variables on each pass of the loop:

forloop.php

```
<html><head><title>For Loop</title></head> <body>
<?php        $a = 0; $b = 0;
             for( $i = 0; $i < 5; $i++ )
             {
                $a += 10; $b += 5;
             }
        echo( "At the end of the loop a=$a and b=$b" );
?>
</body></html>
```

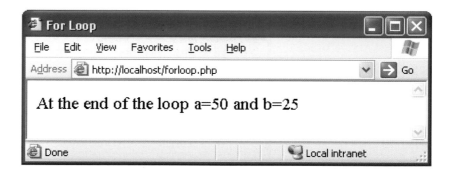

While loop

Another type of loop uses the PHP "while" keyword followed by an expression to be evaluated for a boolean value of true or false.

If the test expression is true then the code in the statement block will be executed. After the code has executed, the test expression will again be evaluated and the loop will continue until the test expression is found to be false.

An infinite loop will lock the script so that the page will not complete.

The statement block must feature code that will affect the test expression in order to change the evaluation result to false at some point, otherwise an infinite loop will be created.

It is important to note that if the test expression is not true when it is first evaluated, the code in the statement block is never executed.

This example decrements a variable value on each iteration of the loop, and the counter increments until it reaches 10, when the evaluation is false and the loop ends.

whileloop.php

```php
<html><head><title>While Loop</title></head>
<body>
<?php        $i = 0; $num = 50;

    while( $i < 10 )
    {
      $num--;
      $i++;
    }
    echo( "Loop stopped at $i<br> \$num is now $num" );
?>
</body></html>
```

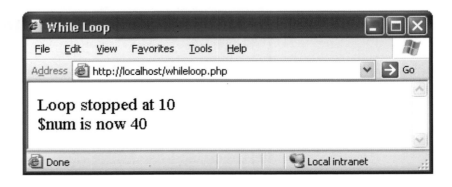

Do–while loop

The PHP "do" keyword is used to denote the start of a "do-while" loop and is followed by a statement block containing the code to be executed on each iteration of the loop.

The statement code is followed by the PHP "while" keyword and an expression to be evaluated for a boolean value of true or false.

If the test expression is true, the loop restarts at the "do" keyword and will continue until the test expression becomes false.

It is important to note that, unlike the simple while loop, the statement code will always be executed at least once by the "do-while" loop because the test expression is not encountered until the end of the loop.

The following example will never loop, because the counter value is incremented to 1 in the first execution of the statement code so the test expression is false the very first time it is tested:

dowhileloop.php

A "while" loop is often more suitable than a "do–while" loop.

```
<html>
    <head><title>Do-While Loop</title></head>
<body>
<?php
    $i = 0; $num = 50;

    do{ $num--; $i++; }
    while ( $i < 1 );

    echo( "Loop stopped at $i<br>\$num is now $num" );
?>
</body></html>
```

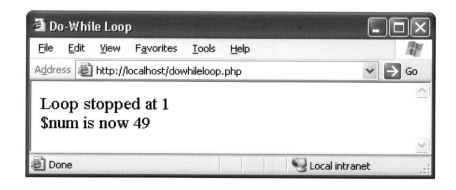

Interrupting loops

The PHP "break" keyword is used to terminate the execution of a loop prematurely.

The "break" statement is situated inside the statement block containing the code that the loop executes, and is preceded by a conditional test.

When the test condition is true, the "break" statement immediately terminates the loop and no further iterations are made.

Notice in the output below that the counter value is still three because the increment in the final iteration is not applied.

In the following example the conditional test becomes true when the counter value reaches three:

break.php

```
<html>
    <head><title>Break Statement</title></head>
<body>
<?php
    $i = 0;

    while ( $i < 6 )
    {
      if( $i == 3 ) break;
      $i++;
    }
    echo( "Loop stopped at $i by break statement" );
?>

</body></html>
```

The "break" keyword is also used as a terminator when used with a "switch" statement – see page 44.

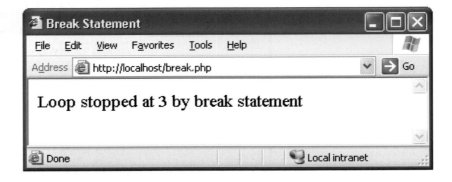

The PHP "continue" keyword is used to halt the current iteration of a loop, but it does not terminate the loop. Just like the "break" statement, the "continue" statement is situated inside the statement block containing the code that the loop executes, preceded by a conditional test.

When the test condition is true, the continue statement immediately stops the current iteration of the loop, but further iterations will be made until the loop ends.

In the example below, the test condition is true when the counter value reaches three, so the string concatenation in that iteration is not applied but the loop continues on.

continue.php

```
<html>
     <head><title>Continue Statement</title></head>
<body>
<?php
     $i = 0; $passes = "";
     while ( $i < 5 )
     {
       $i++;
       if( $i == 3 ) continue;
       $passes .= "$i ";
     }

     echo( "Loop stopped at $i<br>" );
     echo( "Completed iterations:$passes" );
?>
</body></html>
```

The loop counter must be incremented before the continue condition is tested, to avoid creating an infinite loop.

Return statement

The PHP "return" keyword is used in functions to return a final value to the caller of that function.

The example below contains a general purpose function called multiply() that can multiply up to five argument values and return the total to the caller.

It is called from within the echo() function to multiply three argument values. The total is returned, using the "return" keyword, and the echo() function writes the total on the page.

return.php

Each argument to the multiply() function uses a default value of 1 unless another value is passed from the caller. The example illustrated returns the number of minutes in a year, but the function call multiply(365.25,24,60,60) would return the number of seconds in a year.

```php
<?php

    function multiply( $a=1, $b=1, $c=1, $d=1, $e=1 )
    {
      $total = $a * ( $b * ( $c * ( $d * $e ) ) );
      return $total;
    }
?>

<html><head><title>Return Statement</title></head>
<body>
Each year has 365¼ days<br>
Each day has 24 hours<br>
Each hour has 60 minutes<br>
Each year has <?php echo( multiply(365.25, 24, 60) ) ?>
minutes
</body></html>
```

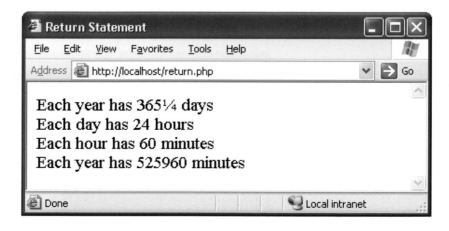

Using arrays

This chapter deals exclusively with the topic of arrays, and illustrates by example what they are and how to use them. The most useful special PHP array functions are demonstrated to show how to store and retrieve values in array structures.

Covers

Chapter Five

Creating an array

An array is a variable that can contain multiple values, unlike a regular variable that contains only a single value. An ordinary variable is given array status by the PHP array() function. Multiple data values can then be assigned to array elements using the array's name together with an element index number. The index starts at zero and the number is placed inside square brackets, as seen here:

array.php

```php
<?php        $arr = array();

             $arr[0] = "First";
             $arr[1] = " PHP ";
             $arr[2] = "array";

             echo( $arr[0] . $arr[1] . $arr[2] );
?>
```

Each array element can now be used like a regular variable.

It is often convenient to specify the initial array values as a list of arguments to the array() function. This is demonstrated in the example below, which creates three arrays. The output from this example, and the one above, is shown at the bottom of this page.

*array.php
(addition)*

```php
<?php        $mo = array( "Jan ", "Feb ", "Mar " );
             $dy = array( "21 ", "22 ", "23 " );
             $yr = array( "2005", "2006", "2007" );

             echo( $mo[1] . $dy[0] . $yr[1] );
?>
```

Remember that array indexing starts at zero. So $arr[2] is the third array element – not the second. See page 59 for how to create index numbering that starts at one instead of zero.

Changing array element values

PHP arrays are very versatile and each element can contain data of a different type.

To demonstrate this feature, the following example creates an array that has three elements initially containing string values. These are written on the page using the **.** dot operator to concatenate the element values into a single string.

Next, new numeric values are assigned to each of the same three elements. The first element is assigned an integer value and the second gets a float value. The total of these is assigned to the third element with the help of the **+** addition operator. Finally, the elements' new values are written out on the page.

chgarray.php

```
<html><head><title>Changing array values</title></head>
<body>
<?php
    #create an array containing 3 strings
    $arr = array( "Red ", "Green ", "Blue" );

    echo( $arr[0] . $arr[1] . $arr[2] . "<hr>" );

    #assign new numeric values
    $arr[0] = 44;
    $arr[1] = 12.5;
    $arr[2] = $arr[0] + $arr[1];

    echo( "$arr[0] + $arr[1] = $arr[2]" );
?>
</body></html>
```

Array elements can also contain boolean values.

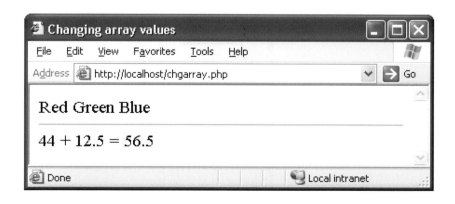

Listing array elements

Retrieving all element values from an array is easy with the PHP foreach() function, which loops through each element of an array.

The value of the element on each iteration of the loop can be assigned to a variable using the PHP "as" keyword. This must be specified as an argument statement to the foreach() function, with the array name and the variable name, using this syntax:

```
foreach( array as variable ) { current-variable-value }
```

The following example loops through an array and writes each element value on the page as an item in an ordered list:

listarray.php

```
<html><head><title>List array values</title></head>
<body> <ol>
<?php
     $arr = array( "Red", "Green", "Blue", "Cyan",
                       "Magenta", "Black", "Yellow" );

     foreach( $arr as $value )
     {
        echo( "<li>Do you like $value ?</li>" );
     }
?>
</ol> </body></html>
```

The foreach() function is especially useful to list the nodes of an XML document – see chapter 14.

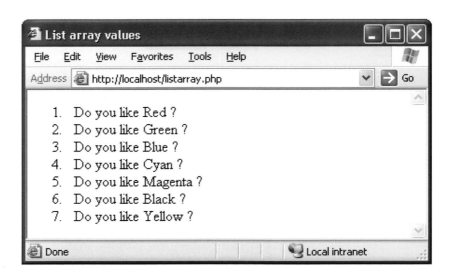

Getting the array size

The PHP sizeof() function is an alias for the PHP count() function, so either can be used to determine the total number of elements in an array. These functions require the name of the array to be specified as their argument.

The PHP script below first create's an empty array, then fills three elements with data using a "for" loop. Each of the element values is written out on the page, using the foreach() function described on the opposite page. Finally, the array size is assigned to a variable and then written on the page.

sizearray.php

```
<html><head><title>Getting array size</title></head>
<body> <ul>
<?php
     $arr = array();

     #assign three element values
     for( $i = 0; $i < 3; $i++ )
     { $arr[ $i ] = "<li>This is element $i</li>"; }

     foreach( $arr as $value){ echo( $value ); }

     #assign the number of array elements
     $size = count( $arr );
     echo("<li>Total number of elements is $size</li>");
?>
</ul></body></html>
```

Notice that the array size expands dynamically to create more elements when needed.

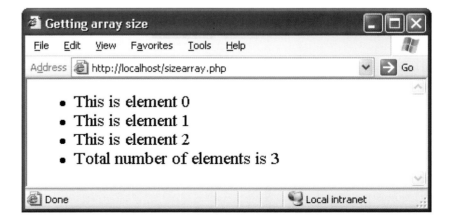

Adding & removing array elements

Additional elements can be created at the beginning of an array using the array_unshift() function, and elements can be added at the end of an array with the array_push() function. Each requires the array name followed by the element data as its arguments.

In the example below, an array is created with just three elements. Two more elements are added at the beginning of the array, then two further elements are added at the end.

addtoarray.php

```
<html><head><title>Adding array elements</title></head>
<body><ol>
<?php
     $arr = array( "Red ", "Green ", "Blue" );

     #add elements at beginning of the array
     array_unshift( $arr, "Cyan", "Magenta" );

     #add elements at end of the array
     array_push( $arr, "Yellow", "Black" );

     #write out each element
     foreach( $arr as $value )
     { echo( "<li>Do you like $value ?</li>" ); }
?>
</ol></body></html>
```

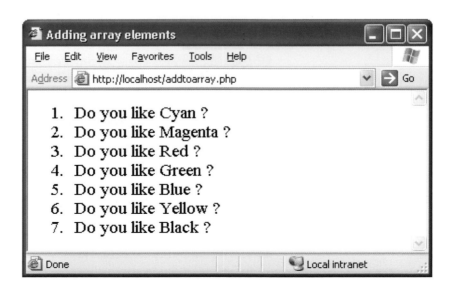

The first element in an array can be removed with the array_shift() function, and the final element can be removed using the array_pop() function. Both these functions return the removed element data, which can be assigned to a variable.

The following example removes the first and last elements from an array, then sorts the remaining elements into alphabetical order using the PHP sort() function.

fromarray.php

```
<html><head><title>Remove array elements</title></head>
<body><ol>
<?php
#create an array containing 5 strings
$arr=array("Orange","Cherry","Apple","Banana","Lemon");

#remove element at beginning of the array
$first = array_shift( $arr );

#remove element at end of the array
$last = array_pop( $arr );

#sort elements alphabetically
sort( $arr );

#write out values
foreach( $arr as $value){ echo( "$value, " ); }
echo( "<br>Removed first element: $first" );
echo( "<br>Removed last element: $last" );
?>
</ol></body></html>
```

Each of the PHP array functions in this example requires the array name to be specified as their argument.

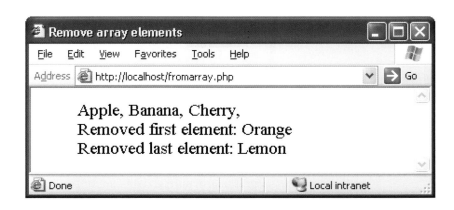

Array keys and values

Instead of a single data value, each PHP array element can contain a key-value pair, where the key can be used in a script to refer to its associated value.

When assigning a key-value pair to an array element, the key name (enclosed in quotes) should come first, followed by "=>" characters and then the value content. It is advisable to use single quotes to surround the key name to differentiate it from a regular string.

To refer to the value, simply use the key name (in quotes) in place of the array index number; for example, $arr['key'].

The example below creates an array with three elements containing key-value pairs. The element content is retrieved, using each key to concatenate its associated value when it is written out on the page.

keyarray.php

```
<html>
<head><title>Key-value array elements</title></head>
<body><ol>
<?php
$arr = array( 'version' => 10,
                    'OS'=> "Linux",'os' => " Mandrake ");
echo
( "Platform:". $arr['OS']. $arr['os']. $arr['version']);
?>
</ol></body></html>
```

Key names are case sensitive, so $arr['OS'] and $arr['os'] refer to different array elements.

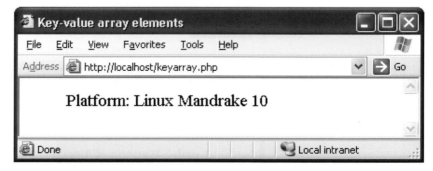

Data submitted from HTML forms takes the input name as a **key** and the input content as its **value**. These can be stored in an array so that user-entered data can be retrieved using the **key** name.

One-based indexing

By default the index of all array elements starts at zero, so that element number one is index number zero. This can be confusing, but PHP does provide a way to start the index at one, so that element number one is also index number one.

The solution is to explicitly specify an integer key of one for the first element value, using the **=>** syntax. All subsequent values will adopt successive index numbers that correctly match their positions in the array.

This technique is demonstrated in the following example, which makes an array containing five elements be indexed as 1-5 instead of the default index numbering of 0-4. Each element value is written out on the page by a loop that can now conveniently refer to each element correctly by its index position.

1basedarray.php

```php
<html><head><title>One-based array index</title></head>
<body><ol>
<?php
 $arr = array( 1 => "1st", "2nd", "3rd", "4th", "5th" );

 for( $i = 1; $i <= sizeof( $arr ); $i++ )
 {
  echo( "Position $i - Element value: $arr[$i]<br>" );
 }
?>
</ol></body></html>
```

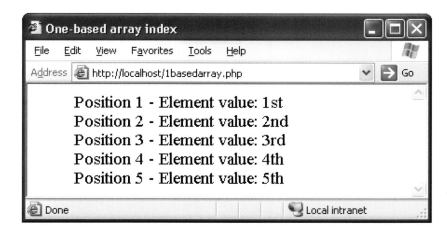

Manipulating arrays

PHP arrays can be easily manipulated by the many special array functions. The array_merge() function allows two arrays to be merged. This requires the two array names as its arguments, and adds the elements of the second array after those of the first array. A specified range of an array's elements can be selected with the array_slice() function, which takes the array name and the start and end positions of the required elements. Array elements can be randomly rearranged with the PHP shuffle() function. The example below demonstrates each of these functions in action.

slicearray.php

```
<html><head><title>Manipulating arrays</title></head>
<body><ol>
<?php $arr1 = array( "Alpha", "Bravo", "Charlie");
       $arr2 = array( "Delta", "Echo", "Foxtrot" );

       $arr = array_merge( $arr1, $arr2 );
       foreach( $arr as $value ) { echo( "$value " ); }
       echo( "<hr>" );

       $arr = array_slice( $arr, 1, 4 );
       foreach( $arr as $value ) { echo( "$value " ); }
       echo( "<hr>" );

   srand( (float)microtime() * 1000000 ); shuffle($arr);
   foreach( $arr as $value ) { echo( "$value " ); }
?>
</ol></body></html>
```

A seed is first provided for the shuffle() function by srand(). For more details please refer to the random number example on page 66.

Generating dynamic content

This chapter demonstrates how PHP can provide dynamic content according to browser type, date and time, randomly generated numbers or user input. It also illustrates string manipulation and how the client browser can be redirected.

Covers

Chapter Six

Identifying browser & platform

PHP creates some useful environment variables, which can be seen on the phpinfo.php page that was used to setup the PHP environment at the beginning of this book; these include an environment variable called HTTP_USER_AGENT, which identifies the user's browser and operating system.

The script below uses the getenv() function to assign a value to this environment variable and then write it out on the page. The illustrations depict the script output in Internet Explorer on Windows XP and in the Mozilla browser on Linux:

identify.php

```
<html>
   <head><title>Get browser &amp; platform</title></head>
<body>
<?php         $viewer = getenv( "HTTP_USER_AGENT" );
              echo( "Browser details:<br>$viewer" );
?>
</body></html>
```

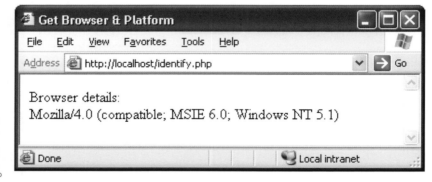

The details in Windows identify Internet Explorer 6.0 as a Mozilla-compatible web browser running on Windows XP (shown as NT5.1). In Linux the genuine Mozilla browser is correctly identified.

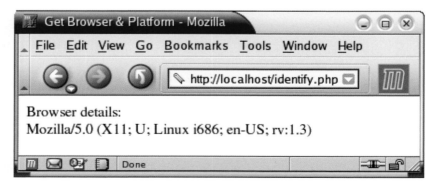

The information contained in the HTTP_USER_AGENT environment variable can be used to create dynamic content appropriate to the browser by using the preg_match() function. This seeks to match a specified string pattern, and has this syntax:

```
preg_match( "/string-to-seek/", "string-to-search" );
```

The following example tries to identify both browser and platform. Default strings are provided for when no match is found. The appropriate string is then written out on the page.

browser.php

```
<html><head><title>Browser content</title></head>
<body>
<?php $viewer = getenv( "HTTP_USER_AGENT" );

     $browser = "an unidentified browser";
     if( preg_match( "/MSIE/i", "$viewer" ) )
          { $browser = "Internet Explorer"; }
     else if( preg_match( "/Netscape/i", "$viewer" ) )
          { $browser = "Netscape"; }
     else if( preg_match( "/Opera/i", "$viewer" ) )
          { $browser = "Opera"; }

     $platform = "an unidentified operating system";
     if( preg_match( "/Windows/i", "$viewer" ) )
          { $platform = "Windows"; }
     else if( preg_match( "/Linux/i", "$viewer" ) )
          { $platform = "Linux"; }

     echo( "You're using $browser on $platform" );
?>
</body></html>
```

The i switch is included in the preg_match() first argument to ensure a case-insensitive search.

Server date & time

The PHP date() function returns the current date and time on the server, formatted according to parameters specified as its arguments. The parameters are indicated by characters listed in the table below and examples are shown at the bottom of this page:

Character	Meaning
a / A	Prints "am" or "pm" / "AM" or "PM"
g / h	Hour in 12-hour format (1-12) / (01-12)
G / H	Hour in 24-hour format (0-23) / (00-23)
i	Minutes (00-59)
s	Seconds (00-59)
Z	Time zone offset in seconds (-43200 to 43200)
U	Seconds since January 1,1970 00:00:00 GMT
j / d	Day of the month (1-31) / (01-31)
D / l	Day of the week (Mon-Sun) / (Monday-Sunday)
w	Day of the week (0-6) from Sunday to Saturday
M / F	Month (Jan-Dec) / (January-December)
n / m	Month (1-12) / (01-12)
y / Y	Year (05) / (2005)
z	Day of the year (0-365)
t	Number of days in a given month (28-31)
S	English ordinal suffix ("th","nd","st")

```
$today = date("M j, Y");        # Dec 10, 2005
$today = date("m.d.y");         # 12.10.05
$time = date("g:i a");          # 5.25 pm
$time = date("H:i:s");          # 05:25:30
```

Time-specific content

The current date or time can be useful to create dynamic content appropriate for the day of the week, month of the year or the time of the day. The example script below writes a message appropriate to the time of the day at which the user accesses the server.

greetings.php

```
<html><head><title>Greetings</title></head>
<body>
<?php  $hour = date( "G" );
        $now = date( "g:i a" );

        $msg = "Good Evening.";
        if( $hour < 18 ) { $msg = "Good Afternoon."; }
        if( $hour < 12 ) { $msg = "Good Morning."; }

        echo( "$msg The time is $now" );
?>
</body></html>
```

This script assesses an integer value of the current hour returned by the date() function. The message displayed may not be appropriate for users from other time zones.

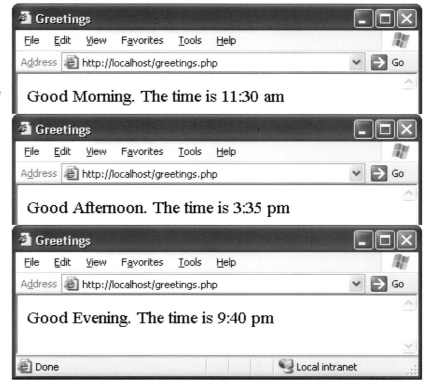

Random number generator

The PHP rand() function is used to generate a random number. Optionally, a range of numbers from which the random number should be chosen can be specified as arguments to the rand() function stating minimum and maximum values of the range. For instance, rand(1,10) would select a number between 1 and 10. When no range is specified the random number will be between zero and the default maximum of 32767.

The random number generator should be seeded to prevent a regular pattern of numbers from being generated. This is achieved using the srand() function, which takes the seed number as its argument. Commonly, the seed number is specified as one million times the current time expressed to microsecond accuracy with the PHP microtime() function.

This example seeds the rand() function in the common manner, then generates two random numbers in the range of 1 to 100.

random.php

```
<html><head><title>Random Numbers</title></head>
<body>
<?php
      srand( microtime() * 1000000 );
      $num = rand( 1, 100 );
      echo( "Microtime:" . microtime() . "<br>" );
      echo( "A random number: " . $num . "<br>" );
      $num = rand( 1, 100 );
      echo( "Another random number:" . $num );
?>
</body></html>
```

The microtime has two parts – the second part is the number of seconds since 00:00:00 January 1, 1970 GMT, and the first part is the microsecond component.

The random number generator is useful to generate different banners on web pages so that the content can change on each visit. The example below generates a random number, then selects a banner image, and associated hyperlink, according to the number.

randompix.php

```
<html><head><title>Random Images</title></head>
<body bgcolor = "#000000" >
<?php
srand( microtime() * 1000000 );
$num = rand( 1, 4 );

switch( $num )
{
case 1 : $car="alfa.jpg";    $url="alfa.php";    break;
case 2 : $car="ferrari.jpg"; $url="ferrari.php"; break;
case 3 : $car="jaguar.jpg";  $url="jaguar.php";  break;
case 4 : $car="porsche.jpg"; $url="porsche.php"; break;
}
$banner = "<a href=\"$url\"> ";
$banner.= "<img src=\"$car\" ";
$banner.= "width=\"380\" height=\"110\" border=\"0\" >";
$banner.="</a>";
echo( $banner );
?>
</body></html>
```

The four banner images and link pages are located in Apache's htdocs folder, alongside the randompix.php file.

In this case the random number chosen was 4 – so the Porsche banner image is displayed and clicking on it would take you to the Porsche page.

Getting form values

PHP is really good at handling data submitted to the server in HTML forms. Each type of HTML form input field sends the data as key-value pairs where the input name is the key, and the input field content is the value.

The simple HTML form shown below contains two text input fields called "username" and "dish", together with a set of radio buttons called "color". Only one radio button may be selected, and its value will be sent to the server when the form is submitted.

fav.html

```
<html><head><title>Your Favorites</title></head>
<body>
<form action="fav.php" method="post">
<b>Please enter your first name:</b>
<input type="text" size="45" name="username"> <br>
<b>Please select your favorite color wine:</b> <br>
<input type="radio" name="color" value="white">  White
<input type="radio" name="color" value="rosé"> Rosé
<input type="radio" name="color" value="red"> Red <br>
<b>Please enter your favorite dish:</b>
<input type="text" size="45" name="dish"> <br> <br>
<input type="submit" value="Submit this form">
</form>
</body></html>
```

Notice that the form's action attribute specifies a form handler named fav.php – this will process the data, and is listed on the opposite page.

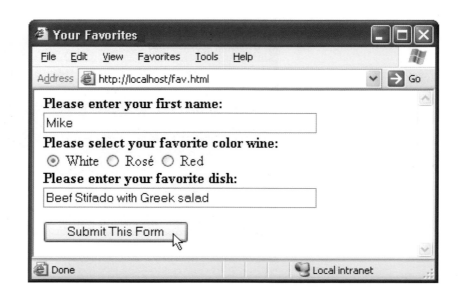

Displaying submitted values

When HTML form data is submitted with the "post" method, PHP adds each submitted key-value pair to its special $_POST[] array. Any submitted value can be referenced by adding its key (input name) within quotes between the square brackets. For instance, the color value in this example can be referenced by $_POST['color'].

The PHP script below begins by assigning each submitted value to a variable, named as its key. The script checks for null values, to ensure user input, then uses the input values in generated output.

Surround the keys with single quotes to differentiate them from text strings, which are surrounded by double quotes.

fav.php

```
<html><head><title>Your submission</title></head>
<body><img src="foodbnr.jpg" width="368" height="54">
<?php
$username = $_POST['username'];        #assign value
$color =    $_POST['color'];           #assign value
$dish =     $_POST['dish'];            #assign value

if( $username != null )
{ echo( "Thanks for your selection $username <hr>" ); }

if( ( $color != null ) && ( $dish != null ) )
{     $msg = "You really enjoy $dish <br>";
      $msg .= "- especially with a nice $color wine";
      echo( $msg ); }
?>
</body></html>
```

The first statement block will be executed only if the user has entered a username value. The second statement block will be executed only if the user has entered both a color and a dish value.

If for some reason the submission method is unknown the values can be referenced from the special $_REQUEST[ ] array in the same way as with $_POST[ ].

Manipulating submitted values

PHP can do much more than simply display values submitted from a HTML form. The submitted data is stored in PHP variables, each keyed against the name of its input field, and these variables can be manipulated by the script, just like other variables.

The HTML form in the example below allows the user to enter two numbers and then select an arithmetical operation to perform on them. When the form is submitted to the server, these values are sent to a PHP form handler called calc.php, listed opposite. The data is associated with the key names of "val1", "val2" and "calc" that have been used for the form's input fields.

calc.html

```
<html> <head> <title>Calculation Form</title> </head>
<body>
<form action="calc.php" method="post">
Value 1: <input type="text" name="val1" size="10">
Value 2: <input type="text" name="val2" size="10"> <br>
Calculation:<br>
<input type="radio" name="calc" value="add">Add
<input type="radio" name="calc" value="sub">Subtract
<input type="radio" name="calc" value="mul">Multiply
<input type="radio" name="calc" value="div">Divide <br>
<input type="submit" value="Calculate">
<input type="reset" value="Clear">
</form>
</body></html>
```

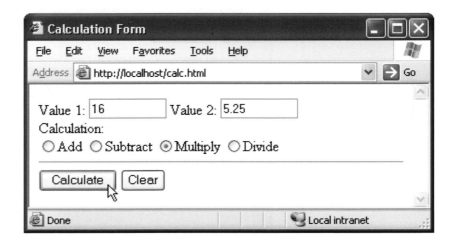

calc.php

```php
<html> <head> <title>Calculation Result</title> </head>
<body>
<?php        $val1 = $_POST['val1'];      #assign value
             $val2 = $_POST['val2'];      #assign value
             $calc = $_POST['calc'];      #assign value
if( is_numeric( $val1 ) && is_numeric( $val2 ) )
{   if( $calc != null )
    {   switch( $calc )
        {
          case "add" : $result = $val1 + $val2; break;
          case "sub" : $result = $val1 - $val2; break;
          case "mul" : $result = $val1 * $val2; break;
          case "div" : $result = $val1 / $val2; break;
        }
      echo( "Calculation result: $result" );
    }
}
else{ echo( "Invalid entry - please retry" ); }
?>
</body></html>
```

The switch statement is seeking a match against the four possible values of the HTML form's radio button set.

The form handler script above uses the PHP is_numeric() function to ensure that two numbers have indeed been entered. This function takes a value to be evaluated as its argument, and returns true only when the value is numeric.

If an arithmetical operation has been selected, a switch statement determines the type of operation and performs the sum. The script then writes out the total of the calculation, or a request to retry if the user has made invalid or incomplete entries.

String manipulation

This example demonstrates how strings can be manipulated using some of PHP's string functions. The function name is sent to the server, when the form is submitted, as the value associated with the key "fcn".

strings.html

```
<html><head> <title>String Manipulation</title> </head>
<body>
<form action="strings.php" method="post">
<b>Enter some text here:</b> <br>
<textarea name="txt" rows="3" cols="45"></textarea><br>
<input type="radio" name="fcn" value="strlen">
Find the text length
<input type="radio" name="fcn" value="strrev">
Reverse the text<br>
<input type="radio" name="fcn" value="strtoupper">
Change to all uppercase
<input type="radio" name="fcn" value="strtolower">
Change to all lowercase<br>
<input type="radio" name="fcn" value="ucwords">
Make the first letter of all words uppercase <hr>
<input type="submit" value="Manipulate">
</form>
</body> </html>
```

The string to be manipulated in this example is the text input content of the textarea, which is sent to the server with the "txt" key.

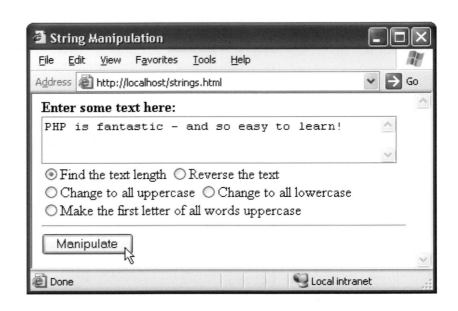

```
<html><head><title>String Result</title></head><body>
<?php        $fcn = $_POST['fcn'];        #assign value
             $txt = $_POST['txt'];        #assign value
             echo( $fcn( $txt ) );                ?>
</body></html>
```

strings.php

The form handler script above takes the function name from the $fcn variable and calls it with the string from the $txt key as its argument. The results of some of the manipulations are illustrated below for the string shown in the textarea on the opposite page.

The strlen() function returns an integer total of the number of characters in a given string.

The strrev() function returns a given string in reverse order.

A given string is returned entirely in uppercase by the function strtoupper() or entirely in lowercase (not illustrated) by the strtolower() function.

The ucwords() function returns a given string with the first letter of each word in uppercase.

Reloading a page

Previous examples have nominated a different file as a form handler to process submitted data, but the same page can be used as the form handler by assigning the PHP environment variable called $_SERVER['PHP_SELF'] to the form's action attribute.

The following example demonstrating this is a guessing game that generates a random number when it is first loaded and assigns it to a hidden form input. The page contains an initial code block that starts with a call to the PHP header() function. Its specified argument of "Cache-Control:no-cache" indicates that the browser should always reload this page, rather than use a cached copy.

The initial code block contains a function called setnum(), which generates a random number between 1 and 20 and assigns it to a variable called $num. Later down the page this value is assigned to the hidden form input called num. When the form is submitted, the page reloads and retains the value of the $num variable. If the user guesses the number correctly, the script calls the setnum() function to assign a new target number to the $num variable.

guess.php

```php
<?php   header( "Cache-Control:no-cache" );

        function setnum()
        {   global $num;
            srand( (double)microtime() * 1000000 );
            $num = rand( 1, 20 );   }
?>

<html><head><title>Number guess</title></head><body>

<?php   $num = $_POST['num']; $guess = $_POST['guess'];
        $self = $_SERVER['PHP_SELF'];   #assign values

if( $num == null )           #starting instructions
{ $msg = "I have thought of a number between 1 and 20";
    $msg .= " <h3>guess what it is...</h3>";
}

#error message for invalid entries
if( $num != null and !is_numeric( $guess ) )
{ $msg = "Your guess was invalid<h3>Try Again!</h3>"; }
```

Notice that the syntax to check for non-numeric entries uses !is_numeric($guess).

guess.php
(continued)

```php
else if( $guess == $num ) #is guess correct ?
{
  if( $num != null )
  {
    $msg = "CORRECT! - THE NUMBER WAS $num";
    $msg .= "<h3><a href = \"$self\" >";
    $msg .= "CLICK HERE TO TRY AGAIN???</a></h3>";
  }
  setnum();                    #set a number number to guess
}
else if( $guess > $num )  #is guess too high ?
{$msg="You guessed $guess<h3>My number is lower!</h3>";}
else if( $guess < $num )  #is guess too low ?
{
 $msg="You guessed $guess<h3>My number is higher!</h3>";
}

echo( $msg );                #write the message out
?>

<form action = "<?php $self ?>" method = "post">
<input type = "hidden" name = "num"
                       value = "<?php echo( $num ); ?>" >
Guess:<input type = "text" name = "guess">
<input type = "submit" value = "Submit">
</form>
</body></html>
```

Because the target number is written as the HTML input value it can be revealed by viewing the source code in the browser.

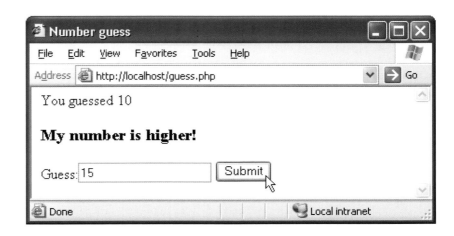

Browser redirection

The PHP header() function supplies raw HTTP headers to the browser and can be used to redirect it to another location. The redirection script should be at the very top of the page to prevent any other part of the page from loading.

The target is specified by using the "Location:" header as the argument to the header() function. After calling this function, the exit() function can be used to halt parsing of the code on that page.

In this example a drop-down selection box offers the user a variety of locations to visit. When the form is submitted, the page is reloaded and the $location variable is used to redirect the browser.

redirect.php

```php
<?php $location = $_POST['location'];   #assign values
      $self = $_SERVER['PHP_SELF'];     #assign values

      if( $location != null )
      {
         header( "Location:$location" ); exit();
      }
?>

<html><head><title>Redirect</title></head>
<body>
Choose a site to visit:
<form action="<?php $self ?>" method="post">
<select name="location">
<option value="http://www.ineasysteps.com">
                     In Easy Steps</option>
<option value="http://www.amazon.com">
                     Amazon</option>
<option value="http://w3c.org">
                     World Wide Web Consortium</option>
<option value="http://www.reuters.com">
                     Reuters News</option>
<option value="http://www.ebay.com">Ebay</option>
</select>
<input type="submit" name="submit" value="Go">
</form>
</body>
</html>
```

The header() function sends a page header to the browser. It must appear at the very start of the page, before any content is sent to the browser.

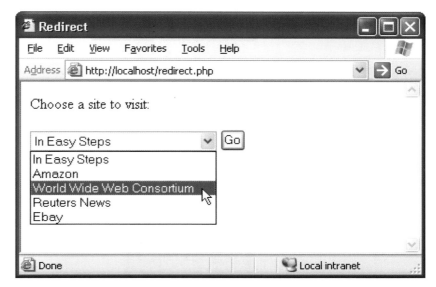

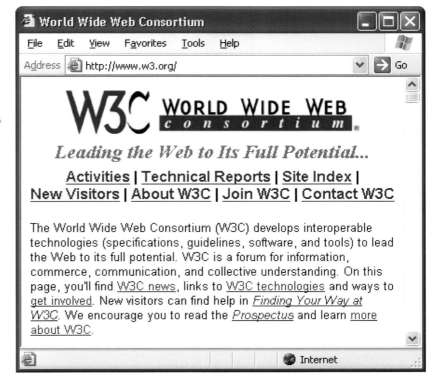

PHP and mobile devices

PHP can be used to supply appropriate content to the emerging range of mobile devices that can access the Internet.

Commonly these have much smaller display areas than a PC monitor, so large images are not suitable. Also they often have reduced capabilities and may not be able to read web pages correctly. For instance, the i-mode standard favored by NTT DoCoMo uses Compact HTML (cHTML), which has only some of the tags available in HTML.

The example below searches the HTTP_USER_AGENT environment variable to identify the browser. If it finds the Pixo micro-browser used on some mobile devices it will supply a small image. Otherwise a large image is supplied.

pixo.php

```
<html><head><title>Welcome Page</title></head><body>
<?php $browser = $_SERVER['HTTP_USER_AGENT'];

if( preg_match( "/Pixo/i", "$browser" ) )
{
  $img = "<img src=\"small-tux.gif\" ";
  $img.= "width=\"64\" height=\"75\" alt=\"tux\" >";
}
else
{
  $img = "<img src=\"large-tux.gif\" ";
  $img.= " width=\"320\" height=\"375\" alt=\"tux\" >";
}
echo( $img );
?>

</body></html>
```

Alternatively, PHP could redirect the micro-browser to a cHTML page containing content appropriate for the device.

File handling with PHP

This chapter demonstrates how PHP can read files and directories and how it can write new files on the server. It also illustrates how to copy, rename and delete files, and then shows how a script can upload files to the server.

Covers

Chapter Seven

Displaying directory files

Special PHP functions can be used to display a list of all the files contained within any directory on your system. Before the directory can be accessed though, it must be opened with the opendir() function. This takes the full path address of the directory as its argument and returns a "directory handle".

Path addresses for Windows locations must have double backslashes because the backslash is used in PHP for escaping.

Once opened, a loop can assign all the file names to a variable list using the readdir() function to step through each in turn; this takes the directory handle as its argument.

It is important to remember to close the directory when the loop has completed, using the closedir() function. Again, this requires the directory handle to be supplied as its argument.

This example assigns each file name in Apache's bin folder in turn to a variable called $file, before adding it to the $file_list variable.

dirlist.php

Notice how the loop checks for a false return from the readdir() function – after the last file name has been read, readdir() returns false and the loop ends.

```php
<?php
    #for Windows...
    $dirname = "C:\\Apache\\bin";

    #(for Linux... $dirname = "/usr/local/apache/bin";)

    $dir = opendir( $dirname );

    while( false != ( $file = readdir( $dir ) ) )
    {
      if( ( $file != "." ) and ( $file != ".." ) )
      {
          $file_list .= "<li>$file</li>";
      }
    }

    closedir( $dir );
?>

<html><head><title>Listing directory</title><head>
<body>
<p>Files in <?php echo( $dirname ); ?> </p>
<ul>
<?php echo( $file_list ); ?>
</ul>
</body></html>
```

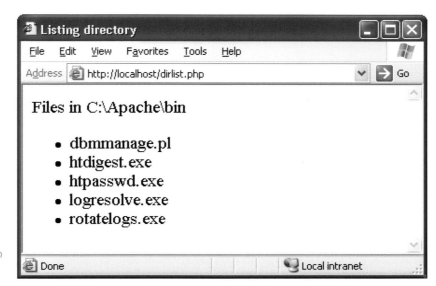

Adjust the code to have the appropriate path for your system. Note that the Linux version of Apache places more files into its bin directory, so a longer list is displayed from the $file_list variable.

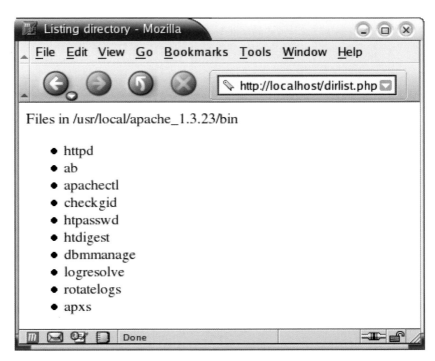

Copying & renaming files

Files on your system can be copied to any location using PHP's copy() function. This requires two arguments: the full path of the source file to be copied, and the full path of the desired location where the copy is to be placed.

When the copy() function succeeds in copying the file it returns a true value, otherwise it returns a value of false.

The example below attempts to copy the error log file from Apache's logs directory, then prints a message describing whether it succeeded or failed.

If the named destination file already exists it will be overwritten by the copy() function.

copyfile.php

```php
<?php # for Windows ...
    $source = "C:\\Apache\\logs\\error.log";
    $dest = "C:\\Documents and Settings\\
                All Users\\Desktop\\error.bak";
    # for Linux ...
    # $source = "/usr/local/apache/logs/error_log";
    # $dest = "/home/mike/Desktop/error_bak";

    if( copy( $source, $dest ) )
    { $msg = "Copied $source<br>to $dest"; }
    else
    { $msg = "Unable to copy $source"; }
?>

<html><head><title>Copying files</title><head>
<body>
<?php echo( $msg ); ?>
</body></html>
```

In Linux ensure that you have permission to write to the target directory.

Files on your system can be renamed using PHP's rename() function. This function requires two arguments: the original name of the file, and the new name to which it will be changed. When the rename() function succeeds in renaming the file it returns a true value, otherwise it returns a value of false.

The example below attempts to rename the copy of Apache's error log file that was created in the example on the opposite page. Upon completion, the script displays an appropriate message describing its success or failure.

renamefile.php

```php
<?php # for Windows ...
    $oldname = "C:\\Documents and Settings\\
                    All Users\\Desktop\\error.bak";
    $newname = "C:\\Documents and Settings\\
                    All Users\\Desktop\\errlog.bak";
    # for Linux ...
    # $oldname = "/home/mike/Desktop/error_bak";
    # $newname = "/home/mike/Desktop/errlog_bak";

    if( rename( $oldname, $newname ) )
    { $msg = "Renamed $oldname<br>as $newname"; }
    else
    { $msg = "Unable to rename $oldname"; }
?>
<html><head><title>Renaming files</title><head>
<body>
<?php echo( $msg ); ?>
</body></html>
```

The rename() function changes the name of an existing file, whereas the copy() function creates a new file with the chosen name.

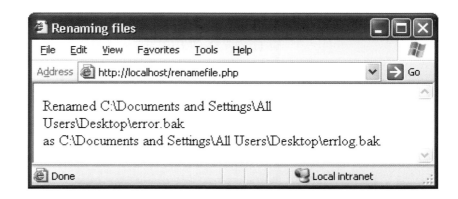

Deleting files

The PHP unlink() function permanently deletes the file specified as its argument (if it is a valid file name).

In this example it appears at the beginning of the code in a custom function that attempts to delete a file and then writes a message confirming if the attempt succeeded or failed. This function is called twice later in the code to attempt to delete two files.

deletefile.php

```php
<?php function try_to_delete( $file )
    { if( unlink( $file ) )
       { echo( "$file<br>has been deleted<hr>" ); }
       else { echo( "Unable to delete $file<hr>" ); }
    }
?>
<html><head><title>Deleting files</title><head> <body>
<?php
$file_A = "C:\\Documents and Settings\\
          All Users\\Desktop\\errlog.bak";
$file_B = "C:\\Documents and Settings\\
          All Users\\Desktop\\errlog.not";
try_to_delete( $file_A );
try_to_delete( $file_B );
?>
</body></html>
```

The attempt to delete the second file fails because the file does not exist. Warning messages can be suppressed by preceding the function name with an @ character in the function call. In this example, @try_to_delete($file_B); would suppress the warning.

Opening & closing files

The PHP fopen() function is used to read text from files, write text to files and append text to files. It requires two arguments: the file name and a mode in which to operate.

File modes can be specified as one of the six options in this table:

The file mode characters represent r for read, w for write, a for append and + for both read and write.

Mode	Purpose
r	Opens the file for **reading** only. Places the file pointer at the **beginning** of the file.
r+	Opens the file for **reading and writing**. Places the file pointer at the **beginning** of the file.
w	Opens the file for **writing** only. Places the file pointer at the **beginning** of the file and truncates the file to zero length. If the file does not exist this will attempt to create it.
w+	Opens the file for **reading and writing**. Places the file pointer at the **beginning** of the file and truncates the file to zero length. If the file does not exist this will attempt to create it.
a	Opens the file for **writing** only. Places the file pointer at the **end** of the file. If the file does not exist this will attempt to create it.
a+	Opens the file for **reading and writing**. Places the file pointer at the **end** of the file. If the file does not exist this will attempt to create it.

If an attempt to open a file fails, fopen() returns a value of false, otherwise it returns a file pointer that references the file. After making changes to the opened file, it is important to close it with the fclose() function to disconnect the file pointer. The fclose() function requires the file pointer as its argument and returns true when the closure succeeds or false when it fails.

The example on the next page demonstrates how to open a file, read the file, then close the file correctly.

Reading a file

A file can be opened with the fopen() function, which requires two arguments specifying the file name and one of the file modes listed on the previous page. The fopen() function returns a file pointer that references the file and can be used to read the file's contents.

The file can then be read with a function called fread(), which also requires two arguments: the file pointer, and the length of the file in bytes.

The file's length can be found using the filesize() function, which takes the file name as its argument and returns the size of the file expressed in bytes.

So the technique to read a file with PHP follows this pattern:

- open the file using **fopen()**

- get the file's length with **filesize()**

- read the file's contents using **fread()**

- close the file with **fclose()**

The following example assigns the contents of a text file to a variable, then displays those contents on the page.

readfile.php

```
<html><head><title>Reading a file</title></head>
<body>

<?php

        $filename = "quote.txt";

        $file = fopen( $filename, "r" );

        $filesize = filesize( $filename );

        $text = fread( $file, $filesize );

        fclose( $file );

        echo( "File Size: $filesize bytes" );
        echo( "<pre>$text</pre>" );
?>
</body></html>
```

quote.txt

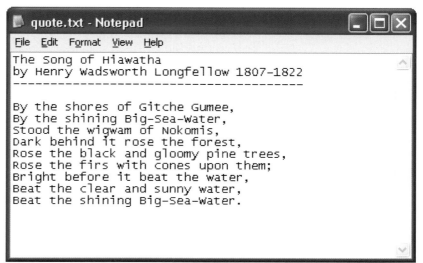

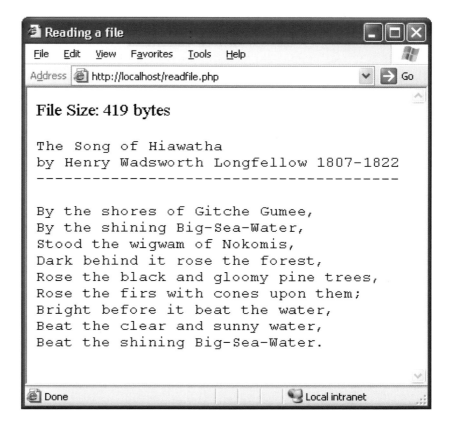

Writing a file

A new file can be written, or text appended to an existing file, using the PHP fwrite() function. This requires two arguments: a file pointer and the string of data that is to be written. Optionally a third integer argument can be included to specify the length of data to write. If the third argument is included, writing will stop after the specified length (in bytes) has been reached.

The file pointer is obtained using the fopen() function with arguments stating the file name and one of the writing file modes listed on page 85.

After writing to a file, it should be closed with the fclose() function, which requires the file pointer as its sole argument.

The existence of a file can be tested with the PHP file_exists() function. This needs the file name as its argument, and will return true if the file is located or false if it cannot be found.

The script below creates a new text file, then writes a short text heading inside it. After closing this file its existence is confirmed.

writefile.php

```php
<?php
    $filename = "C:\\Documents and Settings\\
        All Users\\Desktop\\newfile.txt";

    $file = fopen( $filename, "w");
    fwrite( $file, "Samuel Pepys 1633-1703\n\n" );
    fclose( $file );
?>

<html><head><title>Writing a new file</title></head>
<body>
<?php if( file_exists( $filename ) )
    {
      $file_length = filesize( $filename );
      $msg = "File created at $filename ";
      $msg .= "containing $file_length bytes";
      echo( $msg );
    }
    else { echo( "Unable to create file" ); }
?>
</body></html>
```

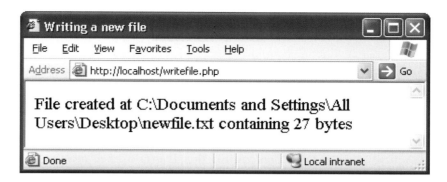

This second script reopens the file created by the first script, then appends a string to the existing heading. Notice that the mode specified to the fopen() function is "w" (write) in the first script but "a" (append) in the second script.

appendtofile.php

Note that these examples use \n to move to a new line and \t to tab across.

```php
<?php
$filename = "C:\\Documents and Settings\\
            All Users\\Desktop\\newfile.txt";

$file = fopen( $filename, "a");

$string = "I went out to Charing Cross, to see Major-
general Harrison hanged,drawn, and quartered, which was
done there, he looked as cheerful as any man could do in
that condition\n\t\tOctober 13,1660";

fwrite( $file, $string );
fclose( $file );
?>
```

newfile.txt

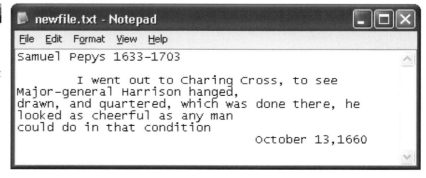

Logging visitor details

The ability to write files makes it simple for PHP to log details about visitors to a web page, and can help website development.

It is especially interesting to discover how visitors arrived at the page, by recording the values of the environment variable HTTP_REFERER. This holds the URL of the page containing the hyperlink that the user followed to get to your page.

The frequency with which visitors return can be discovered by recording the IP addresses of visitors to a page; this is stored in the environment variable REMOTE_ADDR.

The following commented script demonstrates how to log these visitor details, along with their browser type and the time at which they accessed the page.

log.php

```php
<?php
#assign environment variable values
$address = $_SERVER['REMOTE_ADDR'];
$referer = $_SERVER['HTTP_REFERER'];
$browser = $_SERVER['HTTP_USER_AGENT'];

#open the log file
$file = fopen("log.html",  "a");

#write the time of access
$time = date("H:i dS F");
fwrite($file, "<b>Time:</b> $time<br>" );

#write the user's IP address if available
if( $address != null)
{ fwrite($file,"<b>IP Address:</b> $address<br>"); }

#write the URL of the forwarding page if available
if( $referer != null)
{ fwrite($file,"<b>Referer:</b> $referer<br>"); }

#write the user's browser details
fwrite($file,"<b>Browser:</b> $browser<hr>");

#close the log file
fclose($file);
?>
```

The visitor may have typed the address directly into their browser, in which case $_SERVER['HTTP_REFERER'] will not be set.

In this example the log.php file does not have any HTML content, but in reality a regular page would be displayed. A variety of color-coded sample pages have supplied links to log.php and can be clearly identified by opening the log.html log file.

log.html

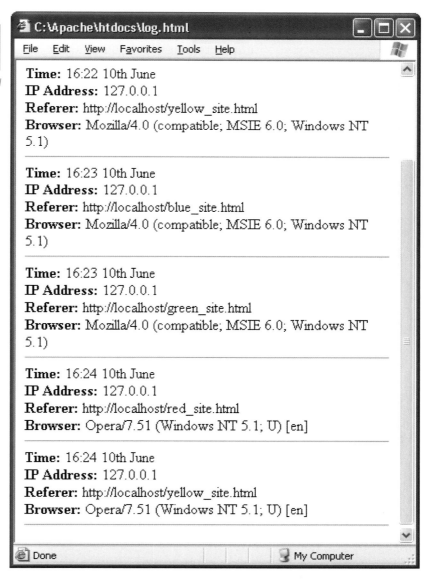

C:\Apache\htdocs\log.html

File   Edit   View   Favorites   Tools   Help

Time: 16:22 10th June
IP Address: 127.0.0.1
Referer: http://localhost/yellow_site.html
Browser: Mozilla/4.0 (compatible; MSIE 6.0; Windows NT 5.1)

Time: 16:23 10th June
IP Address: 127.0.0.1
Referer: http://localhost/blue_site.html
Browser: Mozilla/4.0 (compatible; MSIE 6.0; Windows NT 5.1)

Time: 16:23 10th June
IP Address: 127.0.0.1
Referer: http://localhost/green_site.html
Browser: Mozilla/4.0 (compatible; MSIE 6.0; Windows NT 5.1)

Time: 16:24 10th June
IP Address: 127.0.0.1
Referer: http://localhost/red_site.html
Browser: Opera/7.51 (Windows NT 5.1; U) [en]

Time: 16:24 10th June
IP Address: 127.0.0.1
Referer: http://localhost/yellow_site.html
Browser: Opera/7.51 (Windows NT 5.1; U) [en]

Done   My Computer

Enabling file uploads

A PHP script can be used with a HTML form to allow users to upload files to the server. The remainder of this chapter demonstrates how to create the upload form and the script to process that form.

Initially, files are uploaded to a temporary directory, then relocated to their target destination by a PHP script.

Information in the phpinfo.php page gives the temporary directory that is used for file uploads as upload_tmp_dir, and the maximum permitted size of files that can be uploaded as upload_max_filesize. The default maximum size is 2Mb and the temporary Windows directory is usually C:\temp. These can be modified by editing the php.ini file. In Linux, the temporary directory need not be specified.

The process of uploading a file follows these steps:

- The user opens the page containing a HTML form featuring a text field, a browse button and a submit button

- The user clicks the browse button and selects a file to upload from his or her hard drive

- The full path to the selected file appears in the text field, then the user clicks the submit button

- The selected file is sent to the temporary directory on the server

- The PHP script that was specified as the form handler in the form's action attribute checks that the file has arrived, then copies the file to its intended destination

- The PHP script confirms the success to the user

As usual when writing files, it is necessary for both the temporary and final locations to have permissions set that enable writing – if either are set to be read-only the process will fail.

The upload file used in the example on the following pages is an image file in JPEG format, but could equally have been a text file or any other type of file.

Creating an upload form

The upload form is similar to the forms used in previous examples, but with two important differences. First, the form tag must include an "enctype" attribute with "multipart/form-data" assigned as its value. Second, the form must feature an input of the "file" type, which puts a text field and a browse button on the page.

The HTML code below creates an upload form with all of these features and a submit button.

uploader.html

```
<html><head><title>File Uploader</title></head>
<body> <h3>File Upload</h3>
Select a file to upload:<br>

<form action="uploader.php" method="post"
                    enctype="multipart/form-data">

<input type="file" name="file" size="45">
<br>
<input type="submit" value="Upload File">
</form>

</body> </html>
```

Notice that the form handler to process this form is the uploader.php script assigned to the form's action attribute – this is listed on the next page.

Creating an upload script

When a file is selected for upload, PHP automatically adds it to the special $_FILES environment variable. This is a three-dimensional array that is followed by two set of square brackets with this syntax:

$_FILES['*file-name*' **] [** '*property*' **]**

The upload file can be referenced by inserting its name within quotes in the first set of brackets. Various information about that file can be referenced by inserting properties of "name", "size", "type", "tmp-name" or "error" within quotes in the second set of brackets.

To accommodate the possibility that a file transfer may not complete successfully, the PHP die() function can be used to terminate the execution of a script and display a string specified as its argument.

The example below attempts to copy a file uploaded by the HTML form listed on the previous page to Apache's htdocs directory, and will display the file's details upon completion.

uploader.php

```php
<?php
    if( $_FILES['file']['name'] != "" )
    {
     copy ( $_FILES['file']['tmp_name'],
    "C:/Apache/htdocs/" . $_FILES['file']['name'] )
     or die( "Could not copy file" );
    }
    else{ die( "No file specified" ); }
?>
```

This script also provides a hyperlink that can load the uploaded file into the browser.

```html
<html><head><title>Upload complete</title></head>
<body><h3>File upload succeeded...</h3>
<ul>
<li>Sent: <?php echo $_FILES['file']['name']; ?>
<li>Size: <?php echo $_FILES['file']['size']; ?> bytes
<li>Type: <?php echo $_FILES['file']['type']; ?>
</ul>

<a href="<?php echo $_FILES['file']['name']; ?>">
Click here to view file</a>
</body></html>
```

Uploading a file

Browse to select a file to upload, click on the OK button, then push the form's submit button to upload that file to the server.

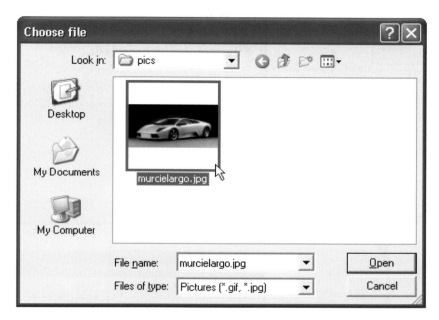

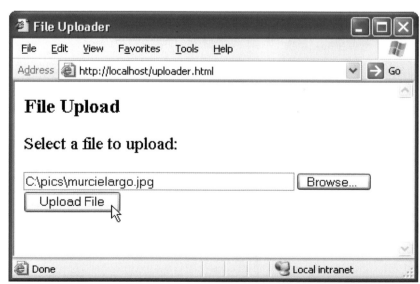

Confirming file upload

When the file has been uploaded, confirmation details are displayed and the user can click the hyperlink to view the uploaded file.

Data persistence

This chapter demonstrates how data can be stored by PHP so that it remains accessible as the user navigates around the various pages of a website. Examples illustrate two possible techniques, employing cookies and session variables. The advantages of each technique are examined.

Covers

Chapter Eight

Introducing cookies

Cookies are text files saved by websites on computers accessing them. Each cookie can contain around 4000 characters, up to 20 cookies can be stored for each website, and the client computer can store a maximum of 300 cookies in total. They are useful to retain user preferences, shopping cart selections, and other snippets of data.

Cookie files can be opened with any text editor, so sensitive information should be encrypted. For instance, rather than directly store a user's password in a cookie, it is better to store a unique identification string that references a database entry containing the password on the server.

When a user has logged onto a site their first name could be stored in a cookie so that each page they visit could greet them by name.

When setcookie() returns true (1) it signifies that the function ran OK – it does not verify that the cookie was accepted.

In PHP, cookies are created with the setcookie() function. This should be called to create a cookie at the very beginning of the PHP document – before any other code, tags or whitespace. The cookie does not become visible until the next page is loaded, but its creation can be verified by the value returned from setcookie(). If successful it returns true (1) otherwise it returns false (0).

cookie.php

```php
<?php
    echo( "Cookie created? : " .
            setcookie( "cookie_name", "cookie_data" ) );
?>

<html>
<head> <title>Cookie</title> </head>
<body></body>
</html>
```

The setcookie() function sets just one cookie at a time and requires up to six arguments. These are described in the following list, in the order in which they must appear:

- **Name** - This sets the name of the cookie and is stored in a PHP environment variable array called $_COOKIE[]. The cookie can be referenced by inserting the cookie name within quotes inside the square brackets.

- **Value** -This sets the value of the named variable and is the content that you actually want to store.

- **Expiry** - This specifies a future time, in seconds since 00:00:00 GMT on January 1st, 1970, at which the cookie will become inaccessible. If this argument is not set, the cookie will automatically expire when the web browser is closed.

- **Path** - This specifies the server directories for which the cookie is valid. A single forward slash character permits the cookie to be valid for all directories. If a directory is specified, the cookie is valid only within that directory.

- **Domain** - This can be used to specify the domain name, and must contain at least two periods to be valid. If this argument is not specified, the default value is the host name of the server that created the cookie. All cookies are valid only for the host and domain that created them.

- **Security** - This can be set to 1 to specify that the cookie should be sent only by secure transmission using HTTPS, otherwise (if set to 0) the cookie can be sent by regular HTTP.

All the arguments except the name argument are optional. If only the name argument is present, the cookie with that name will be deleted from the user's computer.

The expiry argument is easily set by adding a number of seconds onto the current time, retrieved using the PHP time() function. Each of these examples would set a cookie named "ID", with a value of "X12345", to expire 24 hours after it is generated:

```
setcookie( "ID", "X12345", time()+86400 , "/", "", 0 );
setcookie( "ID", "X12345", time()+86400 );
```

The setcookie() function can be used with an expiry date in the past to delete a cookie.

The expiry and security arguments must be integer values. Other arguments can be replaced with an empty string if they are not to be explicitly set.

Set a cookie

Once a cookie has been set, its value can be easily retrieved in PHP simply by referencing the cookie name in the PHP $_COOKIE[] variable array. For instance, the value of a cookie called "data" can be retrieved in PHP scripts with $_COOKIE['data'].

It is important to remember though that the values stored in a cookie cannot be retrieved until the browser makes another HTTP request. This normally means that cookie values stored on page one can be retrieved on only subsequent pages in the website.

The following example demonstrates how to store two items of data entered by the user into form fields called "user" and "color". When the form is submitted, the page reloads. If values have been entered into both form fields, the script stores these values in cookies called "firstname" and "fontcolor" respectively. The browser is then redirected to another page, listed opposite, which retrieves the stored values from within the cookies.

setcookie.php

```php
<?php $user  =  $_POST['user'];          #assign value
      $color = $_POST['color'];          #assign value
      $self  = $_SERVER['PHP_SELF'];     #assign value

      if( ( $user != null ) and ( $color != null ) )
      {
       setcookie( "firstname", $user,  time()+36000 );
       setcookie( "fontcolor", $color, time()+36000 );
       header( "Location:getcookie.php" );
       exit();
      }
?>
<html><head><title>Set Cookie Data</title></head> <body>
<form action="<?php echo( $self ); ?>" method="post">
Please enter your first name:
<input type="text" name="user"> <br> <br>
Please choose your favorite font color: <br>
<input type="radio" name="color" value ="#FF0000">Red
<input type="radio" name="color" value ="#00FF00">Green
<input type="radio" name="color" value ="#0000FF">Blue
<br> <br> <input type="submit" value="submit">
</form>
</body></html>
```

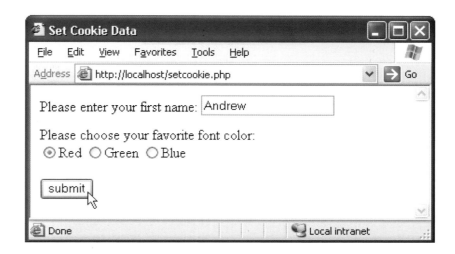

The second page gets the user's preferred font color from the cookie named "fontcolor" and sets the page text to that color in the style sheet. Also the user's name is retrieved from the cookie named "firstname" then written out on the page.

getcookie.php

```php
<?php  $user  = $_COOKIE['firstname'];  #assign value
        $color = $_COOKIE['fontcolor'];  #assign value
?>
<html><head><title>Get Cookie Data</title>
<style type="text/css">
body { color: <?php echo( $color ); ?> }
</style></head>
<body>
<h1>Hello <?php echo( $user ); ?>! </h1>
</body></html>
```

Access limitation

Cookies can be used to prevent direct access to pages of a website without first logging in to that site. The log-in process creates the cookie, then PHP scripts on all other pages confirm the existence of that cookie before displaying their content.

In this example the log-in page creates a cookie called "auth" with a value of "ok" when the user submits the form with both "user" and "pass" input fields completed. The browser is redirected to a second page that seeks the cookie. If that page does not find the cookie, the browser is redirected to the log-in page. Another page in this example makes the same check, and has the same response.

login.php

```php
<?php    $user = $_POST['user'];          #assign value
         $pass = $_POST['pass'];          #assign value
         $self = $_SERVER['PHP_SELF'];    #assign value

         if( ( $user != null ) and ( $pass != null ))
         {
           setcookie( "auth", "ok" );
           header( "Location:loggedin.php" );  exit();
         }
?>
<html><head><title>Set Cookie Data</title></head><body>
<form action="<?php echo( $self ); ?>" method="post">
Name: <input type="text" name="user">
Password: <input type="text" name="pass"> <br><br>
<input type="submit" value="Log Me In"></form>
</body></html>
```

This example makes no attempt to authenticate user name or password – authentication is illustrated in chapter 12.

loggedin.php

```php
<?php $auth = $_COOKIE['auth'];   #assign value
      header( "Cache-Control:no-cache" );
      if( ! $auth == "ok" )
      { header( "Location:login.php" ); exit(); }
?>
<html> <head><title>Logged In</title></head>
<body>You are logged in and can access all pages on this
web site.<br><a href="anotherpage.php"><br>Visit another
page on this site ?</a> </body></html>
```

When you first open a browser, loggedin.php and anotherpage.php cannot be displayed unless you have reached them via the log-in page.

anotherpage.php

```php
<?php $auth = $_COOKIE['auth'];         #assign value
      header( "Cache-Control:no-cache" );
      if( ! $auth == "ok" )
      { header( "Location:login.php" ); exit(); }
?>
<html> <head><title>Still Logged In</title></head>
       <body>You are still logged in... </body> </html>
```

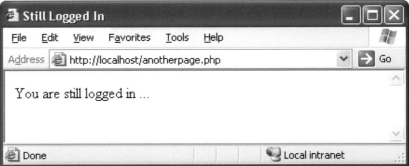

Introducing sessions

An alternative way to make data accessible across the various pages of an entire website is to use a PHP "session".

A session creates a file in a temporary directory on the server where registered session variables, and their values, can be stored. This data will be available to all pages on the site during that visit.

The location of the temporary file is determined by a setting in the php.ini file, called session.save_path. Its current value is shown in the session block of the phpinfo.php page and will probably be set to C:\Windows\temp on Windows or /tmp on Linux systems. The php.ini file can be edited to use a different location if preferred.

When a session is started, a number of things happen:

- PHP first creates a unique identifier for that particular session, which is typically a random string of 32 hexadecimal numbers, such as 8b9e621bc3728ce1165d2fb87ea44f5d

- A cookie called PHPSESSID is automatically sent to the user's computer to store the unique session identification

- A file is automatically created on the server, in the designated temporary directory, and bears the name of the unique identifier prefixed by "sess_". For instance sess_8b9e621bc3728ce1165d2fb87ea44f5d

Now that the session is established, data can be stored in session variables, recorded in the sess_ file on the server.

When a script wants to retrieve the value from a session variable, PHP automatically gets the unique session identifier string from the PHPSESSID cookie, then looks in its temporary directory for the file bearing that name. Once this is located, the file is opened and the value of the variable is recovered.

When the browser closes, or when the session is terminated, the PHPSESSID cookie is automatically deleted.

As this process relies upon only the cookie on the user's computer and the file in the server's temporary directory, the session variables are available to each page of the entire site. The session ends when the user closes their browser or does not load a new page for a predetermined period of time, commonly 30 minutes.

Netscape and Mozilla web browsers have an excellent Cookie Manager facility, which enables you to easily view the cookies stored on your computer. This can be used to verify the existence of a session cookie when a PHP session has been started.

A session must be started before you can find a PHPSESSID cookie - starting a session is described on the next page.

In the Mozilla browser window click Tools > Cookie Manager > Manage Stored Cookies to open the Cookie Manager dialog box. When a PHP session has been started the PHPSESSID cookie will be visible in the Stored Cookies list.

Selecting the PHPSESSID cookie reveals the data it contains in the dialog box's Information field, as shown in the illustration below:

The data in the PHPSESSID cookie shown here matches this file created in the temporary directory:

sess_8b9e621bc3728ce1
165d2fb87ea44f5d

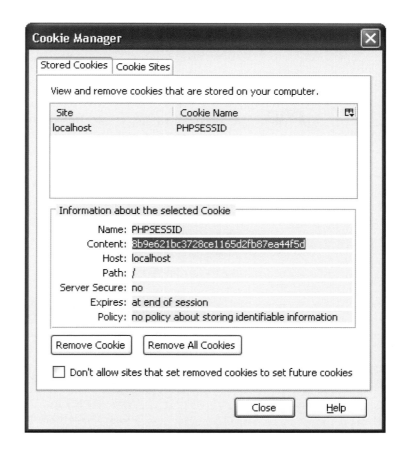

Starting a session

A PHP session is started by making a call to the session_start() function. This first checks to see if a session has already been started, then starts one if none currently exists. It also alerts the PHP engine to expect session variables to be used in the scripts on this page. It is therefore sensible to put the call to session_start() at the beginning of the page.

A session variable is referenced with the PHP $_SESSION[] array variable, by inserting its name within quotes between the square brackets. For instance, $_SESSION['count']=1 initializes a session variable named "count" with a value of 1.

The following example uses the isset() function to first establish if a particular session variable already exists. If it does not, the script creates the session variable named "count". Each time the page is visited during the session, count values gets incremented by 1.

count.php

```php
<?php session_start();    #start a session

# initialize to 1, or increment on subsequent visits
if ( !isset( $_SESSION['count'] ) )
$_SESSION['count'] = 1; else $_SESSION['count']++;
?>
<html><head><title>Count visits</title></head>
<body>
<h2>You have visited this page
<?php echo( $_SESSION['count'] ); ?>
times in this session</h2>
</body></html>
```

Set the option to warn before accepting cookies in order to see when the PHPSESSID cookie is sent to the browser.

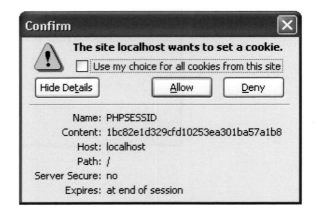

When the page first loads, the value of the "count" variable has been incremented from zero to a value of one. The name and value of this variable are stored in the associated file in the temporary directory on the server. Each time the page is reloaded the value is retrieved from that file, incremented and the new value is stored.

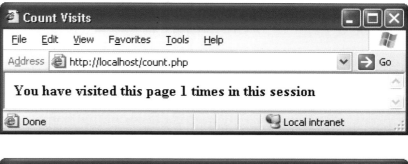

You have visited this page 1 times in this session

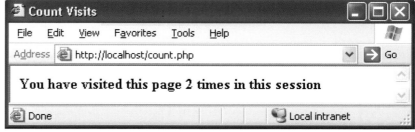

You have visited this page 2 times in this session

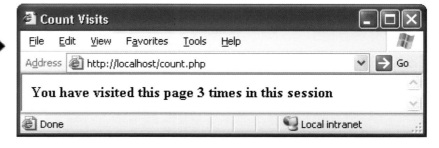

You have visited this page 3 times in this session

Open the file in the server's temporary directory in a text editor to see how the session variable name and value are stored.

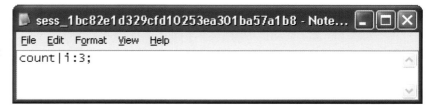

```
count|i:3;
```

Sessions without cookies

The example on the previous page demonstrated how the PHPSESSID cookie is used to store the unique identifier required by the session process. This would seem to duplicate the ability to store and retrieve data directly in cookies.

There is, however, another way to make the unique identifier accessible across an entire website without requiring the browser to accept cookies. This method appends the unique identifier to the URL in each hyperlink to other pages on that website.

This method is more reliable than using cookies: some users prefer to set their browsers to decline cookies, so the intended functionality of the PHP script will not work.

When the unique identifier is found in a PHPSESSID cookie, the SID constant is then set to null.

PHP has a constant called SID that contains details of the unique session identifier as a key-value pair. Here PHPSESSID is the key and the identifier string is the value. This can be simply added to the URL in a hyperlink as a query string. The syntax to do this uses the URL, followed by a question mark, followed by SID, such as:

```
<a href="target.php?<?php echo( SID ); ?>"> link </a>
```

To disable cookies in Netscape/ Mozilla browsers navigate through Edit-Preferences-Privacy & Security-Cookies, then click the radio button option to Disable cookies.

When the link is followed, the session identifier is sent to the target page, thus making the session variables available on that page.

The following example is illustrated using a Mozilla browser with cookies disabled running on Windows. For testing, it is easier to disable cookies in Mozilla than it is in Internet Explorer. The first page starts the session and provides a hyperlink to another page with the SID appended as a query string. The session_id() function displays the the unique identifier part of the SID on both pages.

session_start.php

```
<?php session_start(); ?>

<html><head><title>Session starter</title><head> <body>

<a href="next.php?<?php echo( SID ); ?>">Next page</a>

<hr>

<? echo( session_id() ); ?>

</body></html>
```

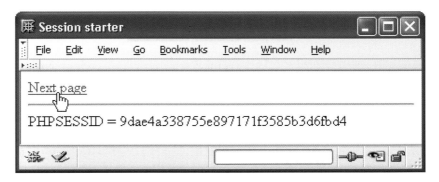

The target page of the link first calls session_start() to continue the current session, then increments a session variable whose value is displayed on the page. A link back to the first page again appends the SID to keep the session alive. Bouncing back and forth between these two pages displays a constant unique identifier on each page and shows an increasing hit count on the second page.

next.php

```php
<?php session_start();
      ($_SESSION['count']) ?
        $_SESSION['count']++ : $_SESSION['count'] = 1; ?>

<html><head><title>Session running</title></head> <body>
<a href="session_start.php?<?php echo( SID ); ?>">Go to
previous page</a><hr>

You have been here <?php echo( $_SESSION['count'] ); ?>
times in this session </body></html>

PHPSESSID = <?php echo session_id(); ?> <br>
```

Setting session preferences

This example demonstrates how to access a user's chosen preference across multiple pages using a session variable called "font". The session ID is passed with the URL links, by appending the SID constant, so that the user's preference can be accessed from any page – even if cookies are disabled.

prefs1.php

```php
<?php session_start();

    if( $_POST['font'] != null )
    {
     $_SESSION['font'] = $_POST['font'];
     header( "Location:prefs2.php?" . SID ); exit();
    }
?>
<html><head><title>Session preferences</title></head>
<body>
<h3>Select Your Preferred Font Family</h3>
<form action="<?php echo( $_SERVER['PHP_SELF'] ); ?>"
                                    method="post">
<input type="radio" name="font" value="serif">Serif
<input type="radio" name="font" value="sans-serif">Sans
<input type="radio" name="font" value="monospace">Mono
<input type="radio" name="font" value="cursive">Cursive
<input type="radio" name="font" value="fantasy">Fantasy
<br>
<input type="submit" value="Submit">
</form>
</body></html>
```

Notice that each of these three pages begins by calling the session_start() function to enable session variables to be used.

When this form is submitted with one of the radio buttons selected, the session variable named "font" gets assigned the chosen button's value and the browser is redirected.

prefs2.php

```php
<?php  session_start(); ?>
<html><head><title>Session running</title>
<style type="text/css">
body { font-family:<?php echo( $_SESSION['font'] ); ?>;}
</style>
</head> <body><h3>Preferred font family is
<?php echo( $_SESSION['font'] ); ?></h3>
<a href="prefs3.php?<?php echo( SID ); ?>">Next page</a>
</body></html>
```

The second page in this example assigns the $_SESSION['font'] variable's value in a style sheet – so that body content is displayed in the font family selected on the first page. The link to another page again appends the SID constant.

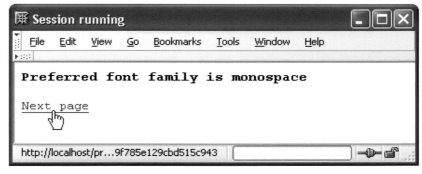

```php
<?php session_start(); ?>
<html><head><title>Session still running</title>
<style type="text/css">
body { font-family:<?php echo( $_SESSION['font'] ); ?>;}
</style>
</head><body><h3>Preferred font family is still
<?php echo( $_SESSION['font'] ); ?> </h3>
<a href="prefs1.php">Change font?</a>
</body></html>
```

prefs3.php

The third page in this example again assigns $_SESSION['font'] in a style sheet – so that body content is displayed in the font family selected on the first page. The link back to the first page simply allows selection of a different font family so does not append the SID.

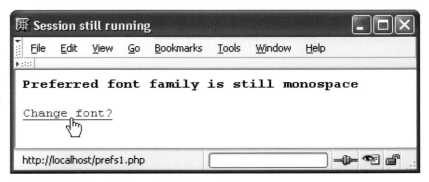

Cookies or sessions?

Cookies are the optimal method for maintaining data with PHP, and it is extremely simple to store the data with the set_cookie() function. Cookies are perhaps easier to use than sessions.

Unfortunately, cookies require the co-operation of the user's browser in allowing cookies to be stored on the client system. As concerns about privacy and security become heightened, with increasing fear of computer viruses, more users than ever are becoming reluctant to allow cookies on their systems. This prevents you from using cookies to store data for PHP routines.

Some of the newly emerging mobile devices that can access the Internet may not even have the capacity to store cookies.

On the other hand, storing data in session variables does not rely upon the user's browser settings, so is far more reliable than using cookies. You just have to remember to append the SID session identifier onto each URL in hyperlinks, and to call the session_start() function at the beginning of each page.

Changing the PHP configuration can even remove the need to call session_start() manually on each page. In the session block of the phpinfo.php page is a directive called "session.auto_start" that by default is set to off on installation.

Save the php.ini file after editing, then restart Apache (as described on page 13) to apply the changes.

Open the php.ini file in a text editor and find the entry for session.auto_start. Change its value from 0 to 1 to turn this feature on. Now PHP will automatically perform the tasks of the session_start() function whenever a page gets loaded.

With session.auto_start set to on, each of the three calls to the session_start() function in the last example can be removed – and the preference data is still maintained as the user navigates between the pages.

Overall it may be better to use sessions rather than cookies, especially to store critical data, such as the selected shopping cart items on an e-commerce website.

Sessions ensure that stored data will be available across the entire website, even in those browsers where cookies are not enabled, but this will use more server resources to store the data.

Sending email with PHP

This chapter features a feedback form on a web page, where visitors can enter comments, which will automatically be sent to a specified email address by PHP. Examples demonstrate how to send plain text messages, HTML-formatted messages and emails with attachments. Error checking is added to prevent the submission of incomplete forms.

Covers

Chapter Nine

Enabling PHP email

PHP must be configured correctly in the php.ini file with the details of how your system sends email. Open php.ini in a text editor, then find the section headed "[mail function]".

Windows users should ensure that two directives are supplied: the first is called SMTP (Simple Mail Transfer Protocol) and defines your email server address; the second is called sendmail_from and defines your own email address.

The configuration for Windows should look something like this:

Installation may have automatically set the necessary directives, but it is still worth checking them.

Linux users simply need to let PHP know the location of their sendmail application. The path, and any desired switches, should be specified to the "sendmail_path" directive.

The configuration for Linux should look something like this:

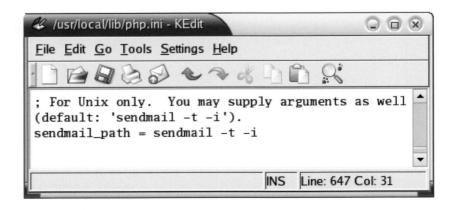

Creating a feedback form

The feedback form shown below is used to submit user data by email in the examples throughout this chapter. It is a HTML page containing a form with three input fields named "username", "useraddr" and "comments". The form submits their values to the form handler (feedback.php) shown on the next page.

feedback.html

```html
<html>
  <head> <title>Feedback Form</title> </head>
  <body>
    <form action="feedback.php" method="post">
      Name:<input type="text" name="username" size="30">
      <br> <br>
      Email:<input type="text" name="useraddr" size="30">
      <br> <br>
      <textarea name="comments" cols="30" rows="5">
      </textarea><br>
      <input type="submit" value="Send Form">
    </form>
  </body>
</html>
```

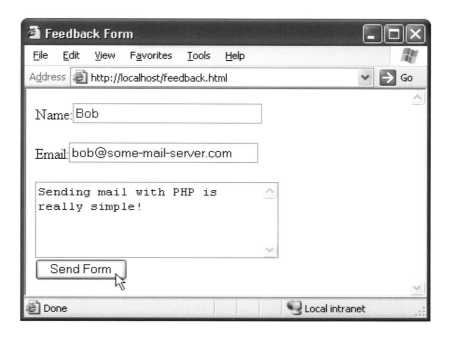

Sending plain text email

The PHP mail() function makes it easy to send email from scripts. This function requires three mandatory arguments that specify the recipient's email address, the subject of the message, and finally the message itself. So the mail() function syntax looks like this:

```
mail( to, subject, message );
```

As soon as the mail() function is called, PHP will attempt to send the email, and return true if it was successful, or false if it failed.

Multiple recipients can be specified by using a comma-separated list as the first argument to the mail() function.

The example that follows is a form handler for the feedback form created on the previous page. It assigns the recipient's address and a subject title to two variables. The user's entry into the feedback form's comment textarea is assigned to a third variable. These variables are then specified as the three arguments to the mail() function when it is called to send the email message.

feedback.php

```php
<?php
    $username = $_POST['username'];    #assign value
    $useraddr = $_POST['useraddr'];    #assign value
    $comments = $_POST['comments'];    #assign value


    $to = "php5ineasysteps@hotmail.com";    #recipient
    $re = "Website Feedback";               #subject
    $msg = $comments;                       #message
    mail( $to, $re, $msg );                 #send mail
?>

<html>
    <head><title>Message Received</title></head>
    <body>
    <h3>Thanks for your comments</h3>
    Message received from <?php echo( $username ); ?>
    <br>
    Reply to <?php echo( $useraddr ); ?>
    </body>
</html>
```

The user's entries into the "username" and "useraddr" fields of the feedback form are used to display a confirmation that the message has been received.

The email message is sent to the address specified as the first argument to the mail() function. Its subject is specified by the second argument. The actual message is specified by the third argument, as illustrated below:

Notice that the sender of this message is that specified to the send_from directive in the php.ini file – not the user's email address.

Sending HTML email

The PHP mail() function optionally accepts a fourth argument, which can be used to specify a string of extra headers to be sent with all emails. Each header must be separated by "\r\n" – representing a carriage return and a newline.

The following example illustrates additions to the feedback form handler to allow HTML formatting by setting the "Content-type:" header to "text/html".

Note that the Cc: header is case-sensitive –CC: or cc: are incorrect.

It assigns the email address entered by the user, in the "useraddr" form field, to the "From:" header. Also, the "Cc:" header is given a second address to which a copy should go.

All header information is contained in the $headers variable, which is specified as the fourth argument to the mail() function.

When a form is submitted, the header information and the message are sent; then a confirmation, like the previous one, is displayed.

*feedback.php
(modified)*

It is essential to set MIME-Version: 1.0 in this example.

```php
<?php $username = $_POST['username'];   #assign value
      $useraddr = $_POST['useraddr'];   #assign value
      $comments = $_POST['comments'];   #assign value

$to = "php5ineasysteps@hotmail.com";    #recipient
$re = "Website Feedback";               #subject
$msg = $comments;                       #message
$headers  = "MIME-Version: 1.0\r\n";    #html headers
$headers .= "Content-type: text/html;";
$headers .= " charset=iso-8859-1\r\n";
$headers .= "From: $useraddr \r\n";            #from
$headers .= "Cc: another@hotmail.com \r\n";    #cc
mail( $to, $re, $msg, $headers );              #send mail
?>
<html>
     <head><title>Message Received</title></head>
     <body>
     <h3>Thanks for your comments</h3>
     Message received from <?php echo( $username ); ?>
     <br>
     Reply to <?php echo( $useraddr ); ?>
     </body>
</html>
```

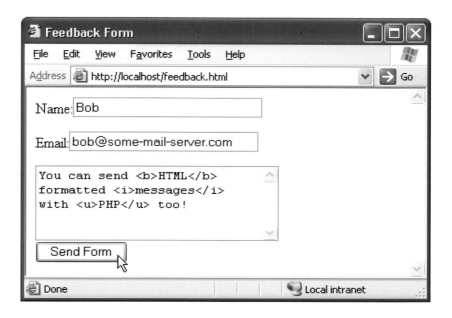

HTML formatting tags can now be included in the user's entry and are applied to the received message. When this form is submitted, the user's comments are received in the format shown below:

Notice that this email appears to be sent from the user's own email address and the Cc: has been added. The From: header has replaced the send_from directive value. Clicking on the reply button will now open a blank email form with the user's own address given as the recipient.

Creating an attachment form

To send an attachment with an email message, an "enctype" attribute must be added to the HTML <form> element and assigned a value of "multipart/form-data".

This example builds on the previous feedback form by adding input fields for subject and file attachment. The user can push the Browse button to open a dialog box that lets them select a file to attach to the message. On submission, the values entered in the fields named "to", "from", "re", "comments" and "att" are sent to the form handler sendmixed.php, listed on page 122.

sendmixed.html

This example puts the inputs inside table cells for better presentation.

```html
<html><head><title>Attachment Form</title></head>
<body>
<form action="sendmixed.php" method="post"
                              enctype="multipart/form-data">
<table>
<tr><td>To:</td>
    <td><input type="text" name="to" size="40"></td>
</tr>
<tr><td>From:</td>
    <td><input type="text" name="from" size="40"></td>
</tr>
<tr><td>Subject:</td>
    <td><input type="text" name="re" size="40"></td>
</tr>
<tr><td>Message:</td>
    <td>
    <textarea cols="30" rows="5" name="comments">
    </textarea>
    </td>
</tr>
<tr><td>Attachment:</td>
    <td><input type="file" name="att" size="26"></td>
</tr><tr><td colspan="2">
    <input type="submit" value="Send Form">
    </td>
</tr>
</table>
</form>
</body></html>
```

...cont'd

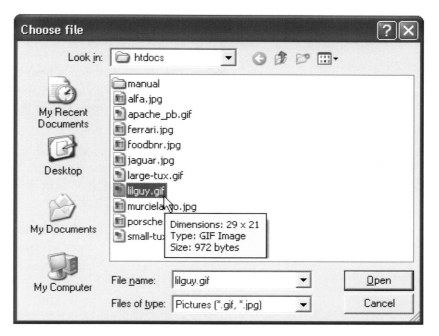

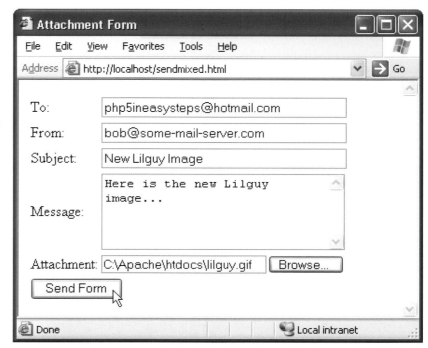

Sending attachments with email

To send an email with mixed content requires a more advanced understanding of email formats. A main Content-Type: header must first declare the content to be "multipart/mixed". Then text and attachment sections can be specified within defined boundaries. Each boundary starts with two hyphens followed by a unique number, which cannot appear in the message part of the email.

It is common to use the PHP md5() function to create a 32-digit hexadecimal number for use in a boundary. The time() function can be specified as its argument to seed the number.

Attached files should be encoded with the base64_encode() function for safer transmission, and are best split into chunks with the chunk_split() function. This adds \r\n inside the file at regular intervals, normally every 76 characters.

The following commented code lists the form handler for the attachment form that was created on page 120:

sendmixed.php

```php
<?php
    $to = $_POST['to']; $from = $_POST['from'];
    $re = $_POST['re']; $comments = $_POST['comments'];

    $att = $_FILES['att'];
    $att_path = $_FILES['att']['tmp_name'];
    $att_name = $_FILES['att']['name'];
    $att_size = $_FILES['att']['size'];
    $att_type = $_FILES['att']['type'];

    #open, read, then close the file
    $fp = fopen( $att_path, "rb");
    $file = fread( $fp, $att_size );
    fclose( $fp );

    #create a boundary string
    $num = md5(time());
    $str = "==Multipart_Boundary_x{$num}x";

    #encode the data for safe transit
    $file = chunk_split(base64_encode($file));

    #define header
    $hdr  = "MIME-Version: 1.0\r\n";
    $hdr .= "Content-Type: multipart/mixed; ";
    $hdr .= "boundary=\"{$str}\"\r\n";
    $hdr .= "From: $from \r\n";
```

The boundary number is assigned to the boundary attribute in the main Content-Type: header.

sendmixed.php
(continued)

The Content-Transfer-Encoding: header for the text is plain "8bit", which is its natural state. The attachment has been encoded with the base64_encode() function so is described as "base64".

The Content-Disposition: header is described here as "attachment" but could alternatively be "inline" to include the attachment in the email message body.

```php
#define message
$msg = "This is a multi-part message in MIME format\r\n\n";
$msg .= "--{$str}\r\n";
$msg .= "Content-Type: text/plain; charset=\"iso-8859-1\"
\r\n";
$msg .= "Content-Transfer-Encoding: 8bit\r\n";
$msg .= "$comments\r\n\n";
$msg .= "--{$str}\r\n";

#define the non-text attachment
$msg .= "Content-Type: {$att_type}; ";
$msg .= "name=\"{$att_name}\"\r\n";
$msg .= "Content-Disposition: attachment; ";
$msg .= "filename=\"{$att_name}\"\r\n";
$msg .= "Content-Transfer-Encoding: base64\r\n";
$msg .= "$file\r\n\n";
$msg .= "--{$str}";

#send mail
$ok = mail( $to, $re, $msg, $hdr );
if( $ok ) echo "OK";
?>
```

Adding error-checking

Previous examples in this chapter have created a form and a separate form handler, but this example combines the feedback form with the form handler script as a single web page.

Assigning the $username, $useraddr and $comments variables to the input fields ensures that any entered values are retained when the form is submitted.

It assigns the $_SERVER['PHP_SELF'] environment variable to the form's action attribute so that the page is reloaded when the form is submitted. The entire HTML form is contained inside a variable named $form, which is written when the page is first loaded. The script ensures that all input fields have been completed before it will send the email, otherwise it will write appropriate error messages and rewrite the form, complete with any entered values. When all input fields have entries, the variable called $valid remains true, so the email is sent and a confirmation is displayed.

combined.php

```
<html><head><title>Combined Feedback Form</title></head>
<body>
<?php #assign form values when applicable
        $username = $_POST['username'];
        $useraddr = $_POST['useraddr'];
        $comments = $_POST['comments'];
        $sent = $_POST['sent'];

#the HTML form that can be written dynamically
$form ="<form action=\"$_SERVER['PHP_SELF']\"
                                        method=\"post\">";
$form.="Name:<input type=\"text\" name=\"username\"";
$form.=" size=\"30\" value=\"$username\" > <br> <br>";
$form.="Email:<input type=\"text\" name=\"useraddr\"";
$form.=" size=\"30\" value=\"$useraddr\"> <br> <br>";
$form.="Comments:<textarea name=\"comments\" ";
$form.="cols=\"30\" rows=\"5\">$comments</textarea>";
$form.="<br> <input type=\"submit\" name=\"sent\" ";
$form.="value=\"Send Form\"></form>";

#execute this code if the form has been submitted once
if($sent)
{ $valid=true;              #set variable default value

  #check username field is not blank
  if( !$username )
  { $errmsg.="Enter your name:<br>"; $valid = false; }
```

if($sent) is equivalent to if($sent==true) and $sent will be null until the form is submitted. Similarly if(!$username) is equivalent to if($username !=null) and $username will be null if the input is empty when the form is submitted.

combined.php
(continued)

```
#check email useraddr field is not blank
if( !$useraddr )
{ $errmsg.="Enter email address:<br>"; $valid=false; }
#check comments field is not blank
if( !$comments )
{ $errmsg.="Enter your comments:<br>"; $valid=false; }
}
```

The $errmsg variable stores any error messages when an incomplete form has been submitted. It is concatenated with the $form variable, containing the entire HTML form, then written on the page.

```
#if invalid write the error message/s and the form
if( $valid != true ){ echo( $errmsg . $form ); }
else  #if the form is valid send the email
{       $to = "php5ineasysteps@hotmail.com";
        $re = "Feedback from $username";
        $msg = $comments;
        $headers = "From: $useraddr \r\n";
        if( mail( $to, $re, $msg, $headers ) )
        { echo("Thanks for your comments, $username");}
}
?>
</body></html>
```

This illustration shows the page after the form has been submitted without any entry in the comments input field.

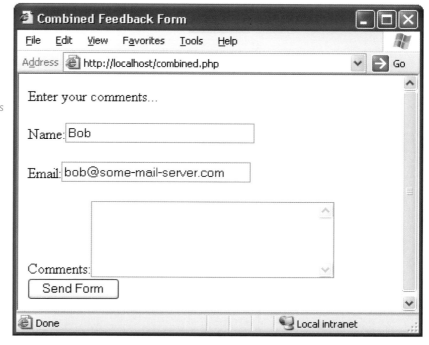

Validating email address formats

PHP's preg_match() function can assess if an email address appears to be in the expected format by matching permitted patterns for each part of the address.

The example on page 124 could be modified with the code below that checks for "@" and "." symbols, and permitted characters.

(modified section for)
combined.php

The trim() function removes any leading and trailing spaces. See page 63 for more about preg_match().

```
if( !$useraddr )
{ $errmsg .="Enter email address:<br>"; $valid = false; }
else
{
  $useraddr = trim( $useraddr );
  #patterns for name,domain and top-level domains
  $_name = "/^[-!#$%&\'*+\\.\/0-9=?A-Z^_`{|}~]+";
  $_host = "([-0-9A-Z]+\.)+";
  $_tlds = "([0-9A-Z]){2,4}$/i";
  #check validity of email format
  if( !preg_match($_name."@".$_host.$_tlds,$useraddr) )
  {
    $errmsg .= "Email address has incorrect format!<br>";
    $valid = false; }
}
```

This illustrates the page after the form has been submitted with an incomplete email address – no top-level domain part.

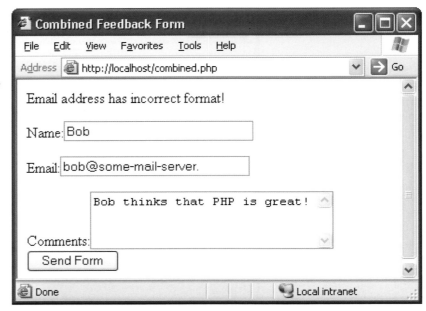

Getting started with MySQL

This chapter illustrates how to store information in a database. It demonstrates some basics of the Structured Query Language (SQL), which is used to add and manipulate data inside databases.

Covers

Chapter Ten

Introducing databases

Databases are simply containers that store data in a structured manner. Every database is composed of one or more tables, which structure the data into organized rows and columns. This makes it easier to reference and manipulate the data.

Each database table column has a label to identify the data stored within the cells in that column. Each row contains an entry called a "record", which places data in each cell along that row.

A typical simple database table looks like this:

```
+-----------+--------+----------+-----------+---------------+
| member_id | fname  | lname    | tel       | email         |
+-----------+--------+----------+-----------+---------------+
|         1 | John   | Smith    | 555-1234  | john@mail.com |
|         2 | Anne   | Jones    | 555-5678  | anne@mail.com |
|         3 | Mike   | McGrath  | 555-3456  | mike@mail.com |
+-----------+--------+----------+-----------+---------------+
```

Column label member_id uses an underscore character because spaces are not allowed in labels.

The rows of a database table are not automatically arranged in any particular order. It is important, therefore, to have some means to identify each record in the table; the example above allocates a member id for this purpose. This unique identifier is known as the "primary key".

Storing data in a single table is very useful, but relational databases with multiple tables introduce more possibilities by allowing the stored data to be combined in a variety of ways. For instance, the following two tables could be added to the database containing the first example table shown above:

```
+----------+--------------+          +-----------+----------+
| video_id | title        |          | member_id | video_id |
+----------+--------------+          +-----------+----------+
|        1 | Titanic      |          |         2 |        1 |
|        2 | Men In Black |          |         1 |        3 |
|        3 | Star Wars    |          |         3 |        2 |
+----------+--------------+          +-----------+----------+
```

The table on the left lists several video titles identified by "video id" number. The table on the right describes a relationship between the tables, linking each member to the video they have rented. So Anne (member #2) has Titanic (video #1), John (member #1) has Star Wars (video #3) and Mike (member #3) has Men In Black (video #2).

Exploring database tables

Open the MySQL monitor in a root shell window, or a Command Prompt window on Windows systems, then type "show databases;" at the mysql> prompt to see all the available databases.

For details on running the MySQL monitor refer back to page 14.

The MySQL installation creates two databases by default – an empty one called "test", and one called "mysql" that is used by MySQL itself. The SQL command "use *database-name*;" selects a database to work with.

Type "use mysql;" to select the mysql database, then type the "show tables;" command to see a list of tables inside that database.

The SQL command "explain *table-name*;" can be used to see the format of a table. This displays all the field names in the table together with details of the data they may contain. Using the mysql database, type "explain user;" to see the format of the user table.

The explain command does not reveal the actual data in the table, but merely the table format – see page 134 to discover how to view the table data.

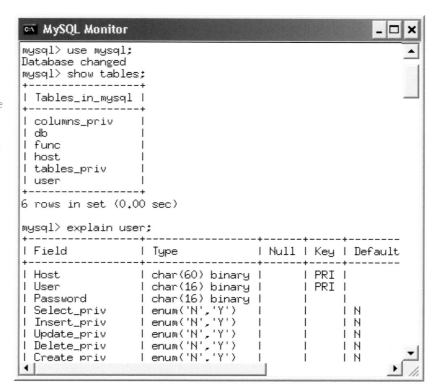

Creating a new database

MySQL databases can be created and their contents amended or queried in the MySQL monitor by using Structured Query Language (SQL) commands.

The SQL command "create database *database-name*;" is used to create a new database.

Open the MySQL monitor then type "create database garage;" to create a new database called "garage".

The MySQL monitor responds by confirming that the new database has been created, with the message Query OK followed by information about affected rows and time elapsed.

The names of all databases on the MySQL server can be viewed with the SQL "show databases;" command to confirm that the new garage database does indeed exist:

In Windows XP the MySQL server can be started, paused and stopped by the Management Console in Control Panel > Administrative Tools > Services.

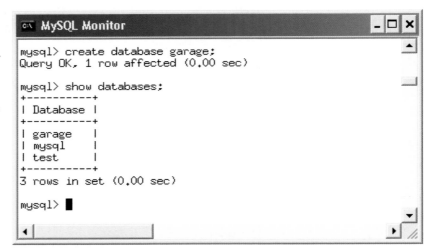

If a database with your chosen name already exists, MySQL will not create a new database, but will respond with this error message:

```
ERROR1007:
Can't create database 'garage'. Database exists.
```

Creating a database table

To create a database table you must first select the database to which it is to be added, using the SQL "use *database-name*;" command. This requires the name of one of the existing databases, revealed by the "show databases;" command.

A semi-colon is required after each complete command.

A new table is created with the SQL "create table *table-name*;" command, specifying a chosen name for that table, then a comma-separated list of chosen column names enclosed within a pair of brackets. Additionally, each column name must be followed by a data type specifier to set the type of data permitted in the table cells of that column. These specifiers can state the SQL keywords of "int" for integer numbers, "decimal" for floating-point numbers, or "text" for character strings.

For instance, the syntax to create a table with three columns is: "create table *table-name* (*column1-name column1-type, column2-name column2-type, column3-name column3-type*);"

Once a database has been selected, the SQL "show tables;" command reveals the names of all tables in that database. This is used in the MySQL monitor illustrated below to confirm the addition of a table called "cars" to the "garage" database created on the facing page. The cars table contains one numeric column called "id", and two text columns called "make" and "model". More SQL column types and table options are described on the next page.

To close the MySQL monitor type "exit" or "quit" at the mysql> prompt.

```
mysql> use garage;
Database changed
mysql> create table cars(id int,make text,model text);
Query OK, 0 rows affected (0.00 sec)

mysql> show tables;
+-----------------+
| Tables_in_garage |
+-----------------+
| cars            |
+-----------------+
1 row in set (0.00 sec)

mysql>
```

SQL data types

The table below describes the range of data type specifiers that can be used when creating table columns in MySQL. It is advisable to specify the permitted data type precisely. For instance, if a column is only going to hold short strings use varchar() rather than text.

Type	Description
int	An integer from -2147483648 to 2147483647
decimal	A floating point number that can specify the number of permissable digits. For example decimal(3,2) allows -999.99 to 999.99
double	A long double-precision floating point number
date	A date in the YYYY-MM-DD format
time	A time in the HH:MM:SS format
datetime	A combined date and time in the format YYYY-MM-DD HH:MM:SS
year	A year 1901-2155 in either YY or YYYY format
timestamp	Automatic date and time of last record entry
char()	A string of defined <u>fixed</u> length up to 255 characters long. For example, char(100) pads a smaller string to make it 100 characters long
varchar()	A string of defined <u>variable</u> length up to 255 characters long that is stored without padding
text	A string up to 65535 characters long
blob	A binary type for variable data
enum	A single string value from a defined list. For example, enum("red","green","blue") allows entry of any one of these three colors only
set	A string or multiple strings from a defined list. For example, set("red","green","blue") allows entry of one or more of these three colors

An enum type can contain up to 65535 permissible elements.

SQL field modifiers

In addition to specifying permissible data types when creating database table columns, the modifiers described in the following table can optionally be stated to further control how a column should be used:

Modifier	Description
not null	Insists that each record must include data entry in this column
unique	Insists that records may not duplicate any entry in this column
auto_increment	Available only for numeric columns to automatically generate a number that is one more than the previous value in that column
primary key()	Specifies as its argument the name of the column to be used as the primary key for that table. For example, primary key(id)

At the MySQL prompt type "explain cars;" to see how the table is defined.

Modifiers could be included when creating the cars table on page 131 to produce a table with better defined columns. The "create table *table-name*;" command shown in the MySQL monitor below can automatically number the primary key id column. Each record must now include data in the "make" and "model" columns, although no duplicate entries are permitted in the "model" column.

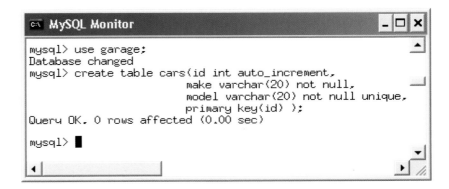

```
mysql> use garage;
Database changed
mysql> create table cars(id int auto_increment,
                         make varchar(20) not null,
                         model varchar(20) not null unique,
                         primary key(id) );
Query OK, 0 rows affected (0.00 sec)

mysql>
```

Inserting table data

Once a table has been created in a MySQL database, data can be entered into it with the SQL "insert into" command. The syntax to enter a complete record across a row is:

"insert into *table-name* values (*value1*, *value2*, *value3*);"

The data values are entered as comma-separated arguments to the SQL values() function; the list must correspond to the number of table columns and each value must be of the correct data type.

Enclose string data inside quotes when inserting data.

Notice that the id value for the second and third records has been generated automatically because of that column's auto_increment modifier.

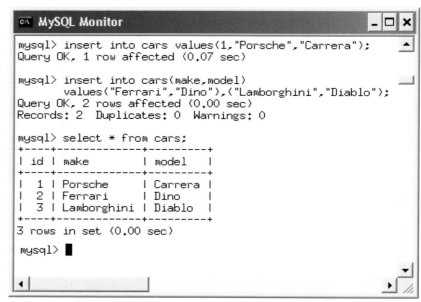

```
MySQL Monitor                                          _ □ ✕

mysql> insert into cars values(1,"Porsche","Carrera");
Query OK, 1 row affected (0.07 sec)

mysql> insert into cars(make,model)
        values("Ferrari","Dino"),("Lamborghini","Diablo");
Query OK, 2 rows affected (0.00 sec)
Records: 2  Duplicates: 0  Warnings: 0

mysql> select * from cars;
+----+-------------+---------+
| id | make        | model   |
+----+-------------+---------+
|  1 | Porsche     | Carrera |
|  2 | Ferrari     | Dino    |
|  3 | Lamborghini | Diablo  |
+----+-------------+---------+
3 rows in set (0.00 sec)

mysql> █
```

Another way to insert data into a table is to specify the column names where the data is to be added as a comma-separated list, such as "insert into *table-name* (*column-name*, *column-name*);". The actual data to be inserted into the specified columns is then listed as the values() function arguments as usual.

SQL instructions in the illustration use both methods to add three records to the "cars" table created on the previous page.

An entire table can be viewed with a SQL "select ★ from" command, followed by the name of the table, and the obligatory semi-colon. The example above uses this command to view the "cars" table.

Altering an existing table

The definition of a column in an existing table can be altered using the SQL commands "alter table" and "modify", with the following syntax:

alter table *table-name* modify *field-name* *type* *modifiers*;

New columns can be added to an existing table using the same "alter table" command, but now with the SQL "add" keyword. The syntax to add an extra column looks like this:

alter table *table-name* add *field-name* *type* *modifiers*;

The example shown in the MySQL monitor below uses the "alter table" command to add a new extra column called "top_mph" to the cars table from the previous page. Data can now be entered into the new column using the SQL "update" command, which is demonstrated on the next page.

The new top_mph column does not have a "not null" modifier, so it is optional to enter data here.

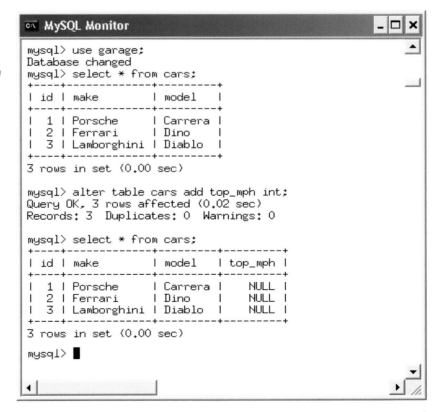

```
mysql> use garage;
Database changed
mysql> select * from cars;
+----+-------------+---------+
| id | make        | model   |
+----+-------------+---------+
|  1 | Porsche     | Carrera |
|  2 | Ferrari     | Dino    |
|  3 | Lamborghini | Diablo  |
+----+-------------+---------+
3 rows in set (0.00 sec)

mysql> alter table cars add top_mph int;
Query OK, 3 rows affected (0.02 sec)
Records: 3  Duplicates: 0  Warnings: 0

mysql> select * from cars;
+----+-------------+---------+---------+
| id | make        | model   | top_mph |
+----+-------------+---------+---------+
|  1 | Porsche     | Carrera |    NULL |
|  2 | Ferrari     | Dino    |    NULL |
|  3 | Lamborghini | Diablo  |    NULL |
+----+-------------+---------+---------+
3 rows in set (0.00 sec)

mysql>
```

Updating records

All data values in an existing table column can be changed using the SQL "update" command with the SQL "set" keyword, like this:

update *table-name* set *field-name* = *new-value*;

More usefully, individual column values can be changed by adding a qualifier to this syntax with the SQL "where" keyword, like this:

update *table-name* set *field-name* = *new-value* where *id* = *int*;

This can be used in the "cars" table example from the previous page to update the "model" and "top_mph" columns:

Notice that id is used as the qualifier with these updates – except for the second and third instructions, which use the value of the make column as their qualifier.

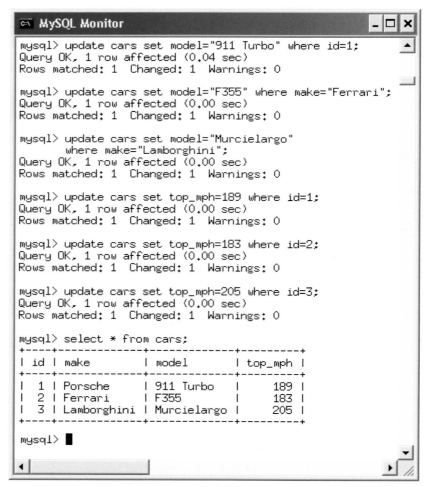

Deleting data, tables & databases

Records can be deleted from a table with the SQL "delete from" command, followed by the table name. This needs to be used with some caution as the command "delete from cars;" would remove all the records from the "cars" table instantly.

Specific records can be deleted from a table by adding a "where" qualifier to the "delete from" command to identify one or more rows. The command to delete the third record in the "cars" table is:

delete from cars where id=3;

Specific columns can be deleted from a table using the SQL "alter table" command followed by the table name, then the "drop" keyword followed by the column name. The command to delete the "top_mph" column from the cars table is:

alter table cars drop top_mph;

A complete table can be deleted from a database using the SQL "drop table" command followed by the table name. So the command to delete the "cars" table is:

drop table cars;

It is always a good idea to use the "show tables;" command to check the contents before using drop database.

An entire database can be deleted with the SQL "drop database" command followed by the database name. The "garage" database, which contained the "cars" table, can be deleted with:

drop database garage;

This deletes the database and also destroys any tables contained within it, so must obviously be used with care.

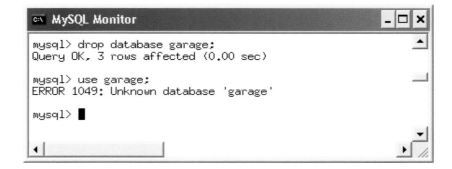

SQL queries

The basic SQL commands demonstrated in this chapter can be used to create database tables and fill them with data. More advanced features of SQL allow the data to be queried for specific information. For instance, the "cars" table at the bottom of page 136 could be searched, to find the details of any car with a top speed exceeding 200 mph, with this query:

select * from cars where top_mph > 200;

In this case there is just one record that fits the bill:

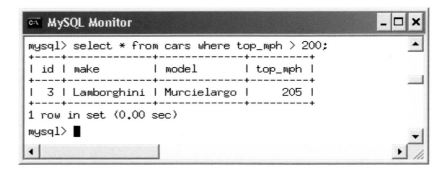

The ability to query data contained within databases is where the power of MySQL lies. More information illustrating the advanced features of the SQL language is given in the manual contained in the Docs folder of the MySQL installation directory.

Further details about SQL can also be found on the Internet in the MySQL Language Reference at www.mysql.com.

MySQL databases can be queried from PHP, using special functions that replicate the SQL commands used in this chapter.

Connecting to a MySQL database from PHP is made easy thanks to the PHP mysql_connect() function. Once connected, the PHP mysql_query() function can be used to query the database and store the results in a PHP variable.

The next chapter demonstrates how to implement all the operations shown in this chapter from inside PHP scripts.

PHP & MySQL together

This chapter demonstrates how to create and manipulate MySQL databases from PHP scripts. The examples perform similar actions to the operations performed directly in the MySQL monitor in the previous chapter.

Covers

Chapter Eleven

Creating a MySQL user & password

The MySQL connection test made at the beginning of this book, right after installation, assumed connection to MySQL as the root user without any password. This affords poor security, so in reality you should create a user with an associated password.

Adding a user is best achieved by entering a "grant statement" into the MySQL monitor as the root user. Opening the MySQL monitor as normal will commonly identify you as the root user. To be sure, from the MySQL monitor type "exit" to close the monitor. Then type this line to open the monitor as the root user:

mysql -u root

The commands are identical in Linux – but remember that you need a root shell window.

Or, if a password has been set up for the root user, the line will be:

mysql -u root -p *password*

Now at the mysql> prompt type this MySQL grant statement:

grant all privileges on *.* to *user-name@domain*
identified by "*password***" with grant option;**

This will create a new user with superuser status – allowing the named user full access from the specified domain, providing that they supply the specified password.

The illustration shows a new user ("mike") being created in the localhost domain, with a simple password of "bingo" – these user details will feature in future code examples in this book.

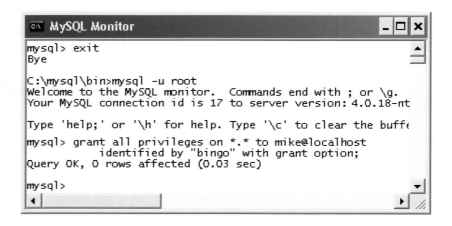

Connecting a user to MySQL

To connect to MySQL the PHP mysql_connect() function requires three arguments specifying valid domain name, user name and password. This function returns true if the connection succeeds, or false if the attempt fails. The script below writes a confirmation if the connection is successful.

connect.php

```php
<?php    $user = "mike";

$conn = mysql_connect( "localhost", $user, "bingo" );
if($conn){
$msg="Congratulations $user, You connected to MySQL"; }
?>
<html><head><title>Connecting user</title></head>
<body><h3> <?php echo($msg); ?> </h3></body></html>
```

The user details are case-sensitive, so changing the value of the $user variable to "MIKE" means that the connection attempt will fail, with a PHP warning message written in the Apache error.log file located in Apache's logs directory; it provides detailed information about the failure, and looks like this:

Listing databases

The equivalent of the SQL "show databases" command in PHP requires the use of three special functions.

First, the mysql_list_dbs() function returns a "result set" of information about all databases, which can be assigned to a variable.

The details of each database are held in separate rows inside the result set, so the total number of databases can be determined using the mysql_num_rows() function to discover how many rows are in the result set. This function takes the result set as its argument.

The name of each database can be extracted from a result set by the mysql_tablename() function. This function is also used to extract the names of each table from a specified database. A result set and row number are required arguments to get the database names.

The example below assigns the result set to a variable called $rs. This is used as the argument to the mysql_num_rows() function to set the length of the loop that lists each database name.

list-dbs.php

Notice that this example uses the @ symbol to suppress warning messages and the die() function to write a message if the connection fails.

```php
<?php
$conn = @mysql_connect("localhost","mike","bingo")
            or die("Sorry - could not connect to MySQL");

$rs = mysql_list_dbs( $conn );
for( $row = 0; $row < mysql_num_rows($rs); $row++ )
{
    $db_list .= mysql_tablename( $rs, $row ) . "<br>";
}
?>
<html><head><title>Listing databases</title></head>
<body><h3> <?php echo($db_list); ?> </h3></body></html>
```

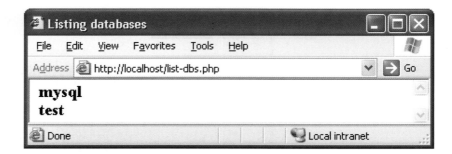

Listing table names

Similar to the mysql_list_dbs() function, the PHP mysql_list_tables() function returns a result set of information about all tables in a database.

Each table name can be extracted by specifying the result set, and its row number in the result set, as the arguments to the mysql_tablename() function. The example below reveals the names of three tables that have been added to the test database.

list-tables.php

MySQL's own database (called "mysql") must be excluded, as its tables cannot be read in this way for security reasons.

```php
<?php $conn = @mysql_connect("localhost","mike","bingo")
       or die( "Sorry - could not connect to MySQL" );

$rs1 = mysql_list_dbs( $conn );
for( $row = 0; $row < mysql_num_rows( $rs1 ); $row++ )
{
  $this_db = mysql_tablename( $rs1, $row );
  $list .= "<b>" . $this_db . "</b><br>";
  if( $this_db != "mysql" )
  {
    $rs2 = mysql_list_tables( $this_db );
    for($num=0; $num < mysql_num_rows($rs2); $num++)
    { $list.= " - ".mysql_tablename($rs2,$num)."<br>"; }
  }
}
?>

<html><head><title>Listing Tables</title></head>
<body> <?php echo( $list ); ?> </body></html>
```

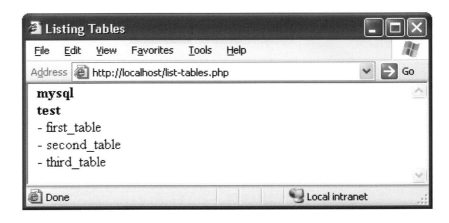

Creating a database

The PHP mysql_create_db() function attempts to create a database with the name supplied as its argument. The example below displays all existing databases, then provides a form where a new database name can be input. When the form is submitted, the script attempts to create a new database with the specified name.

create_db.php

This function returns true if the database is successfully created or false if the attempt fails.

```php
<?php
$conn = @mysql_connect("localhost","mike","bingo")
or die( "Sorry - could not connect to MySQL" );

$rs1 = @mysql_create_db( $_REQUEST['db'] );

$rs2 = @mysql_list_dbs( $conn );
for( $row = 0; $row < mysql_num_rows( $rs2 ); $row++ )
{ $list .= mysql_tablename( $rs2, $row) . " | "; }
?>
<html><head><title>Creating databases</title></head>
<body>
<form action = "<?php echo( $_SERVER['PHP_SELF'] ); ?>"
method="post">Current databases: <?php echo( $list ); ?>
<hr>Name:<input type = "text" name = "db">
<input type = "submit" value = "Create database">
</form></body></html>
```

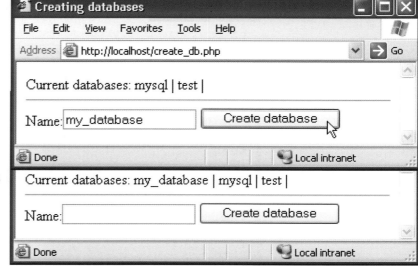

Deleting a database

The PHP mysql_drop_db() function attempts to delete a database with the name supplied as its argument. The example below mirrors that on the facing page but, attempts to delete the specified database when the form is submitted. The function returns true if the attempt succeeds, or false if it fails.

delete_db.php

```php
<?php
$conn = @mysql_connect( "localhost", "mike", "bingo" )
or die( "Sorry - could not connect to MySQL" );

$rs1 = @mysql_drop_db( $_REQUEST['db'] );

$rs2 = @mysql_list_dbs( $conn );
for( $row = 0; $row < mysql_num_rows( $rs2 ); $row++ )
{ $list .= mysql_tablename( $rs2, $row ) . " | "; }
?>
<html><head><title>Deleting databases</title></head>
<body>
<form action="<?php echo( $_SERVER['PHP_SELF'] ); ?>"
method="post">Current databases: <?php echo($list); ?>
<hr>Name:<input type = "text" name = "db">
<input type = "submit" value = "Delete database">
</form></body></html>
```

Notice how the @ symbol is used to suppress warnings.

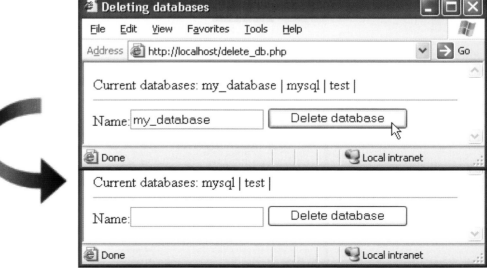

Creating a database table

An existing database can be selected for use with the PHP mysql_select_db() function, which takes the database name and connection link as its two arguments. Once selected, operations can be performed by specifying SQL commands as arguments to the PHP mysql_query() function. So "create table *table-name*" can be used to create a new table inside a database.

An SQL command specified in PHP does not need the semi-colon terminator that is required when entering SQL commands directly in the MySQL monitor.

This example creates an interface to dynamically create a new database table. Initially $fields is not set, so a form is written asking how many columns are required. When the form is submitted, the script generates a form with inputs for the names and data types of each field. The values entered into each field of the completed form are used to produce a SQL command to create a database table with the chosen fields.

create_table.php

```
<html><head><title>Creating a table</title></head><body>
<?php          $self = $_SERVER['PHP_SELF'];
               $fields = $_POST['fields'];
               $db =       $_POST['db'];
               $name =     $_POST['name'];
               $table =    $_POST['table'];
               $type =     $_POST['type'];
               $size =     $_POST['size'];
```

When this first form is submitted with an entry in the input field the $fields variable is set, so the script moves onto the next section.

```
if( !$fields and !$db )
{$form ="<form action=\"$self\" method=\"post\">";
 $form.="How many fields are needed in the new table?";
 $form.="<br><input type=\"text\" name=\"fields\">";
 $form.="<input type=\"submit\" value=\"Submit\">";
 echo( $form ); }
```

The second form allows you to enter the name of an existing database to use, a name for the new table, column names with permissible data types, and, optionally, field sizes.

create_table.php
(continued)

```php
else if( !$db )
{
 $form ="<form action=\"$self\" method=\"post\">";
 $form.="Database:
          <input type=\"text\" name=\"db\"><br>";
 $form.="Table Name:
          <input type=\"text\" name=\"table\"><br>";

for ( $i = 0 ; $i < $fields; $i++ ) { $form.=
  "Column Name:<input type=\"text\" name=\"name[$i]\">";
$form.="Type: <select name=\"type[$i]\">";
$form.="<option value=\"char\">char</option>";
$form.="<option value=\"int\">int</option>";
#...plus options for all other possible data types...
$form.="</select> ";
$form.="Size:<input type=\"text\" name=\"size[$i]\">"; }

$form.="<input type=\"submit\" value=\"Submit\">";
$form.="</form>"; echo( $form );
}
```

The drop-down selection box can be expanded to include options for all possible field data types – see page 132.

This form generates the appropriate number of field inputs from the value entered in the first form. When this completed form is submitted, the $db variable is found to be set so the process moves on to the concluding section of the script, which is listed on the next page.

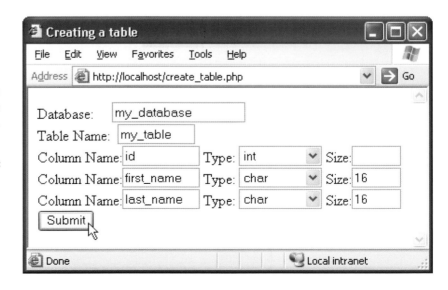

create_table.php
(continued)

This is the real business section of the script – it connects to MySQL, selects the specified database, builds an SQL query from the data entered in the previous form, then executes the query. The complete SQL command is displayed for reference, and a confirmation is written.

You can also now see this new table in the MySQL console.

```
else
{ #make the connection to mysql
  $conn = @mysql_connect("localhost", "mike", "bingo")
                    or die("Err:Conn");
  #select the specified database
  $rs = @mysql_select_db($db, $conn) or die("Err:Db");
  #create the query
  $sql = "create table $table (";
  for ($i = 0; $i < count($name); $i++)
  { #field name & data type
    $sql .= "$name[$i] $type[$i]";
    #allow size specification for char and varchar types
    if(($type[$i] =="char") or ($type[$i] =="varchar"))
    { #if a size has been specified add it to the query
      if($size[$i] !="" ){ $sql.= "($size[$i])"; }
    }
    #if this is not the final field add a comma
    if(($i+1) != count($name) ){ $sql.=","; }
  } $sql .= ")";
  #display the SQL query
  echo("SQL COMMAND: $sql <hr>");
  #execute the query - attempt to create the table
  $result = mysql_query($sql,$conn) or die("Err:Query");
  #confirm if successful
  if ($result)
  { echo("RESULT: table \"$table\" has been created"); }
}
?> </body> </html>
```

Inserting table data

Adding record data to a database table employs the same technique that was used to create a new table in the previous example. The table is selected with the mysql_select() function, then an SQL query containing the record data is supplied as the argument to the mysql_query() function. This uses the SQL command "insert into *table-name*" followed by each piece of field data.

This example allows data to be entered into the my_table table that was created in the previous example:

add_record.php

```
<html><head><title>Add record to my_database/my_table
</title></head><body>

<?php          $self =  $_SERVER['PHP_SELF'];
               $id =    $_POST['id'];
               $fname = $_POST['fname'];
               $lname = $_POST['lname'];   ?>

<form action="<?php echo( $self ); ?>" method="post">
ID: <input type="text" name="id" size="3">
First Name: <input type="text" name="fname" size="8">
Last Name: <input type="text" name="lname" size="8"><br>
<input type="submit" value="Submit"> </form>

<?php
if( $id and $fname and $lname ) #ensure values exist
{ #connect to mysql
  $conn=@mysql_connect( "localhost", "mike", "bingo" )
                              or die( "Err:Conn" );
  #select specified database
  $rs = @mysql_select_db( "my_database", $conn )
                              or die( "Err:Db" );
  #create the query
  $sql="insert into my_table (id, first_name, last_name)
          values ( $id, \"$fname\", \"$lname\" )";
  #execute the query
  $rs = mysql_query( $sql, $conn );
  #confirm the added record details
  if($rs){ echo( "Record added:$id $fname $lname" ); }
}
?>
</body></html>
```

In the list of SQL query values any string data should be surrounded by escaped quotes, as shown here.

The execution of this script is illustrated on the next page.

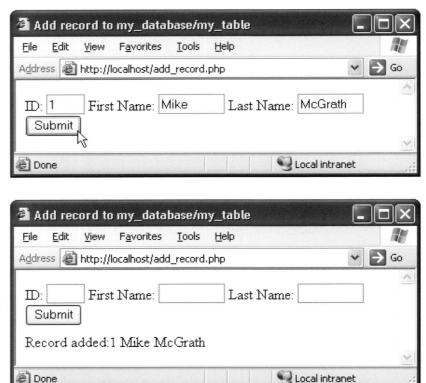

When the form is submitted, a confirmation is written showing record details that were entered into the table. The illustration below shows the table in the MySQL console, using the SQL "select * from *table-name*" command after adding more records.

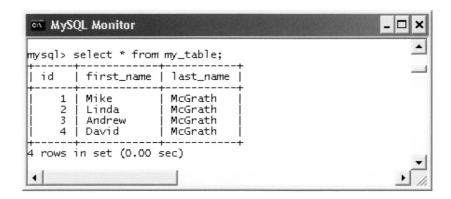

Altering tables

Existing table column properties can be changed with the SQL command "alter table *table-name* modify *column-name property*".

The script below alters the my_table table on the facing page to restrict the "id" column to numbers containing at most three digits. Similarly, it extends the permissible character length of the column named "last_name" from 16 characters to 32 characters.

alter_table.php

```php
<?php

#connect to MySQL
$conn = @mysql_connect( "localhost", "mike", "bingo" )
                                    or die( "Err:Conn" );
#select the specified database
$rs = @mysql_select_db( "my_database", $conn )
                                    or die( "Err:Db" );

#create then execute the 1st query
#reduce field to 3 number length
$qry = "alter table my_table modify id int(3)";
$rs = mysql_query( $qry, $conn ) or die("Err:Query 1");

#create then execute the 2nd query
#extend field to 32 character length
$qry = "alter table my_table modify last_name char(32)";
$rs = mysql_query( $qry, $conn ) or die("Err:Query 2");

?>
```

The alter statements must include the columns' data types or the column specifications will not be modified.

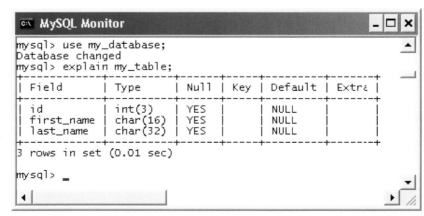

```
mysql> use my_database;
Database changed
mysql> explain my_table;
+------------+----------+------+-----+---------+-------+
| Field      | Type     | Null | Key | Default | Extra |
+------------+----------+------+-----+---------+-------+
| id         | int(3)   | YES  |     | NULL    |       |
| first_name | char(16) | YES  |     | NULL    |       |
| last_name  | char(32) | YES  |     | NULL    |       |
+------------+----------+------+-----+---------+-------+
3 rows in set (0.01 sec)

mysql>
```

Check the new table format in the MySQL monitor to see that the modifications have been applied.

Retrieving data from a table

Data can be retrieved from a MySQL database using the SQL command "select *field-names* from *table-name*" to specify the fields required and the name of the table to search.

The PHP mysql_fetch_array() function returns an associative array of all the requested data from the table, row by row. This function requires the query result set as its argument. Each piece of data in the array is associated to the column name. The data is best assigned to an array variable using a while loop so that the data for each row can be retrieved using its associated column name on each iteration.

The following example retrieves the data from two columns of the my_table table, shown on page 150. Each iteration of the loop assigns a row's data to an array called "$row", then the value associated with the column first_name for each row is written out.

get_data.php

```php
<html><head><title>Get data</title></head>
<body>
<?php
#connect to MySQL
$conn = @mysql_connect( "localhost", "mike", "bingo" )
                     or die( "Err:Conn" );

#select the specified database
$rs = @mysql_select_db( "my_database", $conn )
                     or die( "Err:Db" );

#create the query
$sql="select id, first_name from my_table";

#execute the query
$rs = mysql_query( $sql,$conn );

#write the data
while( $row = mysql_fetch_array( $rs ) )
{
   echo( "ID: " . $row["id"] );
   echo(" - FIRST NAME: " . $row["first_name"] ."<br>");
}
?>
</body></html>
```

SQL queries that work in the MySQL monitor can be used as the first argument to the PHP mysql_query() function.

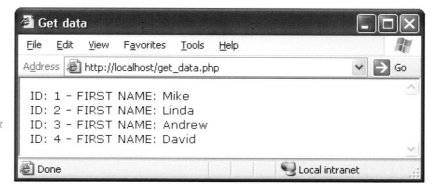

Data order can be specified by adding an "order by" clause to the end of the SQL query. Adding "order by first_name" to the end of the query opposite arranges the data alphabetically by first_name:

The method of working with MySQL via PHP follows this pattern –
1) connect to MySQL
2) select a database to use
3) build a SQL query
4) execute the query
5) make use of the returned result set data.

Specific data can be retrieved by adding a **where** qualifier to the SQL query. For instance, adding **where id=3** to the query in the code shown opposite retrieves data from only that row:

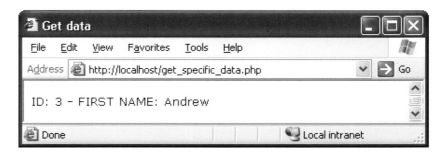

More MySQL

The common basic database operations demonstrated in this chapter use just some of the features of MySQL. To discover ways to make MySQL even more flexible it is recommended that you download the MySQL manual.

The manual is available from the MySQL website at http://mysql.com/documentation, or one of its mirror sites.

As testimony to the widespread popularity of MySQL, the manual is available in many languages, and in a variety of formats including HTML, Windows HLP format, PostScript, TexInfo and PDF.

A tutorial is included in the manual, together with examples illustrating common database queries – but, of course, these give only SQL code and do not feature any PHP scripts.

The MySQL website at http://mysql.com gives the latest news on the development of MySQL and posts details about forthcoming developers' conferences. It also offers a number of interesting User Stories, where you can read how other people are using MySQL.

If you would prefer to work with MySQL via a Graphical User Interface (GUI), rather than from a command line, try the MySQLGUI program available at http://mysql.com/downloads. There are versions for both Windows and Linux.

Help with MySQL is available from the MySQL forum on the Developer Shed website at http://forums.devshed.com. It is worthwhile reading through past questions and answers to get a flavor of the forum before posting any questions yourself – and you may find the answer to your question is already there.

The main Developer Shed website at www.devshed.com is a great resource for learning more about MySQL, as it features lots of articles submitted by developers. Many of these are in the form of a tutorial or discussion and often relate the story of a problem that was overcome using both MySQL and PHP together.

User authentication

This chapter demonstrates how to create a PHP log-in routine. The user name and password entered on the log-in page are authenticated against a list of valid user names and passwords stored in a MySQL database.

Covers

Chapter Twelve

Creating a user table

It is useful to restrict access to parts of a website by requiring visitors to enter a user name and password for authentication against a list of authorized users. A PHP script could verify the input against a list stored in a text file, but it is faster and more efficient to maintain the list in a database table.

In this case the table will need to have four columns to store the user's first name, last name, user name and password. The table can be created using the create_table.php script described in the previous chapter on pages 146–148.

First specify that four fields are needed, then submit the form.

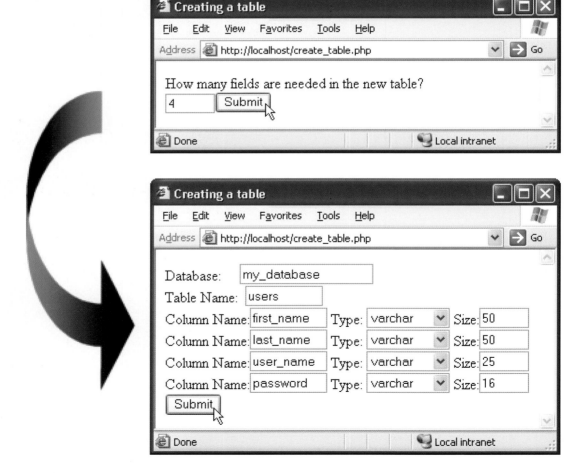

Next, enter the name of the database to use and specify the new table name as "users". Type the four field names "first_name", "last_name", "user_name" and "password" into the input fields and change each data type to "varchar". Set the field lengths to 50 for the real names and just 25 for the user name. Allow a length of 16 for the password field because MySQL will store password information in encrypted form as a 16-digit hexadecimal number.

Now submit the form to create the "users" table.

When the completed form is submitted, the SQL query creates the new table and the page displays a confirmation. The new users table can be viewed in the MySQL monitor to confirm its format.

To ensure that all user names are unique, alter the table to modify the user_name column – as shown in this illustration.

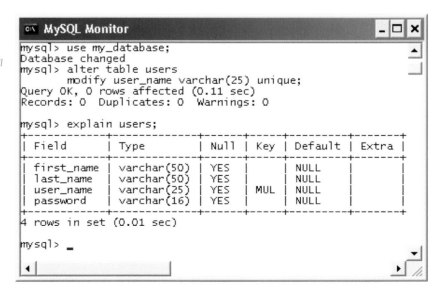

Adding authorized users

A form can be used to add details of each new user to the "users" database table that was created on the previous page. Each of four text inputs correspond to the table's four fields and are named "firstname", "lastname", "username" and "password".

When the page is first loaded, an if-else statement in the PHP script tests to see if values exist for each of these text inputs. If not, the script dynamically writes a form where their values can be entered. The section of the script containing the form is listed below:

add_user.php

The PHP variables are assigned to the value attributes of each input so that if an incomplete form is submitted any text input that was completed will retain its original entry.

```php
<html><head><title>Adding a User</title></head><body>
<?php        $self =       $_SERVER['PHP_SELF'];
             $firstname =  $_POST['firstname'];
             $lastname =   $_POST['lastname'];
             $username =   $_POST['username'];
             $password =   $_POST['password'];

if( ( !$firstname ) or ( !$lastname )
                 or ( !$username ) or ( !$password ) )
{
 $form ="Please enter all new user details...";
 $form.="<form action=\"$self\"";
 $form.=" method=\"post\">First Name: ";
 $form.="<input type=\"text\" name=\"firstname\"";
 $form.=" value=\"$firstname\"><br>Last Name: ";
 $form.="<input type=\"text\" name=\"lastname\"";
 $form.=" value=\"$lastname\"><br>User Name: ";
 $form.="<input type=\"text\" name=\"username\"";
 $form.=" value=\"$username\"><br>Password: ";
 $form.="<input type=\"text\" name=\"password\"";
 $form.=" value=\"$password\"><br>";
 $form.="<input type=\"submit\" value=\"Submit\">";
 $form.="</form>";
 echo( $form );
}
```

When the fully completed form is submitted, the script moves on to the else block, listed opposite. This connects to MySQL and selects the user table, then inserts each of the text input values into the appropriate columns. A confirmation is written for the new user.

add_user.php
(continued)

```
else
{ $conn = @mysql_connect( "localhost", "mike","bingo" )
    or die("Could not connect to MySQL"); #connect MySQL
  $db = @mysql_select_db( "my_database", $conn )
    or die("Could not select database"); #select database
  $sql = "insert into users
    (first_name,last_name,user_name,password) values
    (\"$firstname\",\"$lastname\",\"$username\",
      password(\"$password\") )";        #create the query
  $result = @mysql_query( $sql, $conn )
    or die("Could not execute query"); #execute the query
  if( $result ) { echo( "New user $username added" ); }
}
?> </body></html>
```

The password() function used here is not PHP – it's a MySQL function that encrypts the password as a 16-digit hexadecimal number.

Remember to surround the form variables with escaped quotes inside the SQL query.

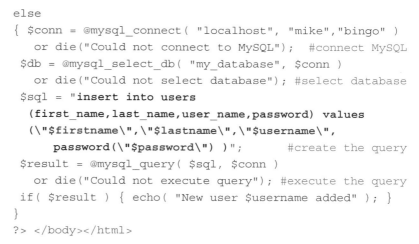

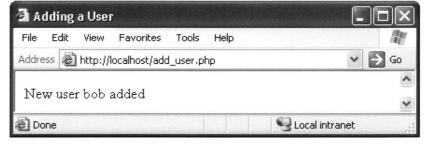

Displaying authorized users

The add_user.php interface from the previous page has been used to add a total of 10 users to the "users" database table that was created at the beginning of this chapter.

Complete details of each user can be retrieved from the users database table and displayed in a HTML table.

This script uses the SQL "select ★ from *table-name*" command to collect the entire data from the users database table.

A variable called $list is used to build a string containing a complete HTML table. This starts with a row of column headings for First Name, Last Name, User Name and Password. Each row of the users database table is then added to the string as a row in the HTML table. Once the HTML table is complete, it is written out on the page to display all the users' details.

get_users.php

```php
<html><head><title>Get Users</title></head>
<body>

<?php

#connect to MySQL
$conn = @mysql_connect( "localhost", "mike", "bingo" )
            or die( "Could not connect" );

#select the specified database
$rs = @mysql_select_db( "my_database", $conn )
            or die( "Could not select database" );

#create the SQL query
$sql = "select * from users";

#execute the query
$rs = mysql_query( $sql, $conn )
            or die( "Could not execute query" );

#start building a HTML table for the users' details
$list = "<table border=\"1\" cellpadding=\"2\">";
$list .= "<tr><th>First Name</th>";
$list .= "<th>Last Name</th>";
$list .= "<th>User Name</th>";
$list .= "<th>Password</th></tr>";
```

get_users.php
(continued)

```php
#loop through each row of the users database table
while( $row = mysql_fetch_array( $rs ) )
{
  $list .= "<tr>";
  $list .= "<td>".$row["first_name"]."</td>";
  $list .= "<td>".$row["last_name"]."</td>";
  $list .= "<td>".$row["user_name"]."</td>";
  $list .= "<td>".$row["password"]."</td>";
  $list .= "</tr>";
}
$list .= "</table>";

#write out the list of users
echo( $list );

?>
</body></html>
```

Notice that the passwords are reproduced in the 16-digit hexadecimal format created by the MySQL password() function.

Get Users

File   Edit   View   Favorites   Tools   Help

Address http://localhost/get_users.php   Go

First Name	Last Name	User Name	Password
Robert	Evans	bob	6a8d554d1f478f65
Sandra	Rhodes	sandy	6a03ed4d0af1d409
Tom	Barring	tommy	74eaa64766b00a8b
Ann	Sanderson	annie	2dfcc51b188b83ac
Geoff	Clark	clarky	181f163946e81997
Barbara	Melling	barbie	04155ced02005602
Gary	Truman	gaz	6c863b722925665f
Maureen	Harris	mo	780722fe164bc509

Done   Local intranet

The user log-in form

A typical log-in page asks that the user's name and password should be entered into form text inputs. When the form is submitted, these values can be checked by PHP against a table of authorized users.

The simple HTML page listed below names the input fields as "username" and "password" and their values are retrieved by the PHP script opposite in variables named $username and $password.

authenticate.html

The form's action attribute is assigned the name of the script on the opposite page as its form handler.

```
<html><head><title>Log-In Page</title></head>
<body>
Please enter your user details to log-in here...

<form action = "authenticate.php" method = "post">
Username:<br>
<input type = "text" name = "username">
<br><br>
Password:<br>
<input type = "text" name = "password">
<br><br>
<input type = "submit" value = "Log In">
</form>

</body></html>
```

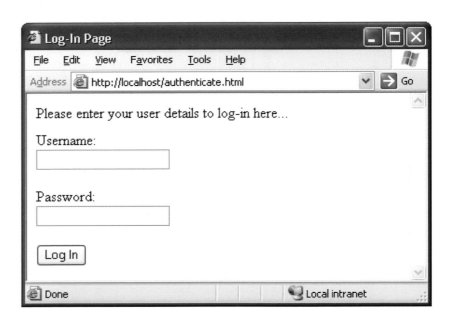

The log-in form handler script

The form handler script for the log-in form opposite first checks that there are entries in both "username" and "password" fields. If so, the script looks in the "users" database table, created earlier in this chapter, and seeks matches to the $username and $password values. The number of table rows that do match is stored in a variable called $num. An if-else statement block then tests to see that at least one row matched, and will either create a confirmation message or return the browser to the log-in page, depending on the result. If the log-in succeeds, a welcome message is written out.

authenticate.php

Notice how the $referer variable is used to specify the address of the log-in page.

A successful log-in attempt is illustrated on the next page.

```php
<?php          $username = $_POST['username'];
               $password = $_POST['password'];
               $self =    $_SERVER['PHP_SELF'];
               $referer = $_SERVER['HTTP_REFERER'];

#if either form field is empty return to the log-in page
if( ( !$username ) or ( !$password ) )
     { header( "Location:$referer" ); exit(); }
#connect to MySQL
$conn = @mysql_connect( "localhost", "mike", "bingo" )
                    or die( "Could not connect" );
#select the specified database
$rs = @mysql_select_db( "my_database", $conn )
          or die( "Could not select database" );
#create the SQL query
$sql="select * from users where user_name=\"$username\"
     and password = password( \"$password\" )";
#execute the query
$rs = mysql_query( $sql, $conn )
          or die( "Could not execute query" );

#get number of rows that match username and password
$num = mysql_numrows( $rs );
#if there is a match the log-in is authenticated
if( $num != 0 )
{ $msg = "Welcome $username - your log-in succeeded!"; }
else #or return to the log-in page
{ header( "Location:$referer" ); exit(); }
?>
<html> <head><title>Log-In Authenticated</title></head>
<body> <?php echo( $msg ); ?> </body> </html>
```

An authenticated log-in attempt

The log-in page illustrated below shows user entries in the form text fields of authenticate.html that is listed on page 162. The username matches that of the user named Robert Evans in the first row of the users database table, shown on page 161.

When encrypted by the MySQL password() function the value in the password field will also match that of the user named Robert Evans. The form handler script, authenticate.php – listed on the previous page, will find a match for these values on one row of the "users" database table so this log-in attempt will succeed.

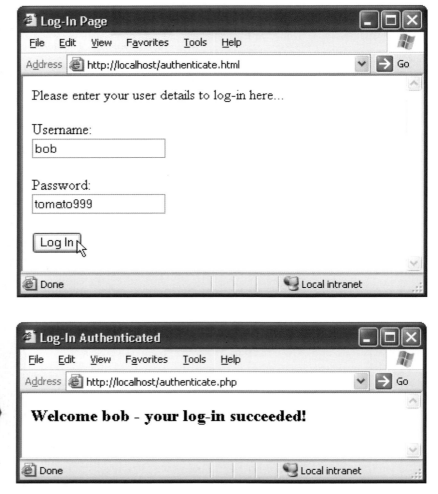

A PHP guestbook

This chapter demonstrates a popular application of PHP: a guestbook for a website, where visitors can leave comments. These are stored in a MySQL database and can be retrieved at any time for viewing in chronological order on a single page.

Covers

Chapter Thirteen

Creating a guestbook database table

A guestbook application first requires a database table to store the messages that visitors will leave. This can be created directly in the MySQL monitor, or with a PHP script.

The following script uses the existing database "my_database". There it creates a table called "guestbook" with fields for "id", "name", "email address", "comments" and an automatic timestamp entry of the date and time that the message was recorded.

This script needs to be run just once to build the guestbook table.

guestbook-create.php

The 14–digit timestamp represents year(4), month(2), day number(2), hours(2), minutes(2) and seconds(2) – in that order. For more details see page 171.

```php
<html>
<head> <title>Create guestbook table</title> </head>
<body>

<?php

   #connect to MySQL
   $conn = @mysql_connect( "localhost", "mike", "bingo" )
           or die( "Could not connect to database" );

   #select the database
   $rs = @mysql_select_db( "my_database", $conn )
           or die( "Could not select database" );

   #create the SQL query
   $query = "id int(4) auto_increment,";
   $query.= "name varchar(50),";
   $query.= "email varchar(50),";
   $query.= "comments text,";
   $query.= "time timestamp(14), primary key(id)";

   $sql = "create table guestbook( $query )";

   #execute the query
   $rs = @mysql_query ($sql)
      or die("<h3>Could not create guestbook table <br>
                          Does it already exist?</h3>");

   #confirm the result
   echo( "<h3>Created guestbook table</h3>" );
?>
</body> </html>
```

You can confirm the format of the guestbook table in the MySQL monitor with the explain guestbook; *SQL command.*

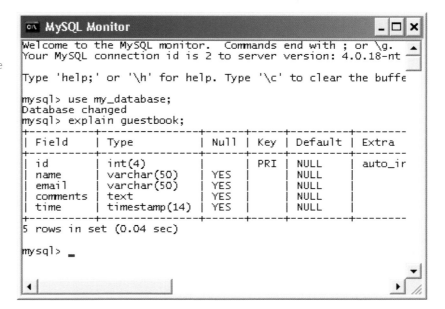

Subsequent attempts to run this script will fail because the guestbook table has already been created.

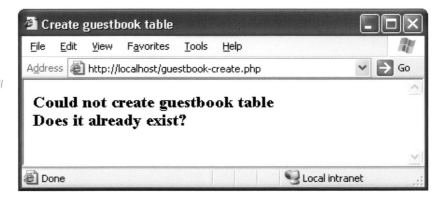

Signing the guestbook

Once the "guestbook" database table has been created, by the script on the previous page, data can be stored in it by submission from a HTML form using PHP. When first loaded in a browser the following PHP script displays a form containing fields for "name", "email" and "comments". Upon submission, the form will be displayed once more if any of the three fields are blank.

If the form has been completed correctly, the script will add the input entries to the corresponding columns of the guestbook database table. The page will display a confirmation and provide a hyperlink to another page where the guestbook data can be seen.

guestbook-sign.php

```php
<html><head><title>Sign the guestbook</title></head>
<body>
<?php       $self =      $_SERVER['PHP_SELF'];
            $name =      $_POST['name'];
            $email =     $_POST['email'];
            $comments =  $_POST['comments'];
            $submit =    $_POST['submit'];
#the html form
$form = "<form action=\"$self\" method=\"post\">";
$form.= "Name: <input type=\"text\" name=\"name\" ";
$form.= "size=\"50\" value=\"$name\"> <br>";
$form.= "Email: <input type=\"text\" name=\"email\" ";
$form.= "size=\"50\" value=\"$email\"> <br>";
$form.= "Comments:<br>";
$form.= "<textarea name=\"comments\" cols=\"45\" ";
$form.= "rows=\"4\">$comments</textarea> <br>";
$form.= "<input type=\"submit\" name=\"submit\" ";
$form.= "value=\"Sign\"> </form>";

#on first opening display the form
if( !$submit){ $msg = $form; }
#or redisplay a message and the form if incomplete
else if( !$name or !$email or !$comments)
{ $msg = "<b>Please complete all fields</b><br><br>";
  $msg.= $form; }
#or add the form data to the guestbook database table
else #otherwise connect to MySQL
{ $conn = @mysql_connect( "localhost", "mike", "bingo" )
  or die( "Could not connect to database" );
```

When the page is first loaded the $submit variable will not exist.

guestbook-sign.php
(continued)

```php
#select the database
$rs = @mysql_select_db( "my_database", $conn )
    or die ( "Could not select database" );

#create the SQL query
if( $name and $comments )
{
  $sql ="insert into guestbook (name, email, comments)
          values(\"$name\",\"$email\",\"$comments\")";
  $rs = @mysql_query( $sql, $conn )
          or die ( "Could not execute SQL query" ); }

#confirm entry and display a link to view guestbook
if($rs)
{ $msg = "<h3>Thank you - your entry has been saved.";
  $msg.= "<br><a href = \"guestbook-view.php\">";
  $msg.= "View My Guestbook</a></h3>"; }
}

#write the page
echo( $msg );
?>
</body></html>
```

This illustration shows the form redisplayed after submission of an incomplete form – there is no entry in the comments field. Notice that the previous entries are retained by assigning their PHP variable values to the form's HTML value attributes. A successful submission is illustrated on the next page.

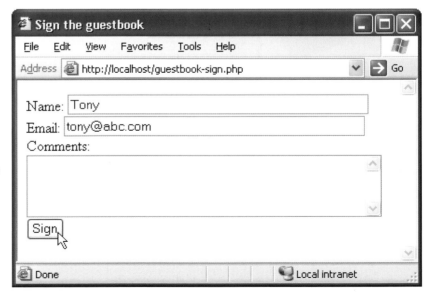

Inserting guestbook entries

When the form created by the script on the previous page is submitted with entries in all fields, the data is added to the guestbook database table and a confirmation is displayed.

The record can now be viewed in the MySQL monitor. Notice that data is added automatically to the id and time fields.

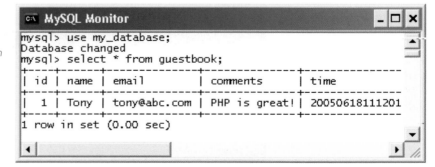

Using timestamp data

The MySQL 14-digit timestamp number records the date and time, where the first four numbers are the year, then each successive pairs of numbers are the month, day number, hour, minutes and seconds.

The PHP substr() function can be used to return a part of a timestamp specified as its first argument. Its second argument states the required starting character position as an integer, and its third argument specifies the character length of that substring.

timestamp.php

```
<html><head><title>Using timestamp</title></head> <body>
<?php
$conn = @mysql_connect( "localhost", "mike", "bingo" );
$rs =   @mysql_select_db( "my_database", $conn );
$sql =  "select * from guestbook where id=1";
$rs =   @mysql_query( $sql, $conn );

#split the timestamp into organized date format
while ( $row = mysql_fetch_array( $rs ) )
{
  $datetime = $row["time"];
  $year = substr( $datetime, 0, 4 );
  $mon  = substr( $datetime, 4, 2 );
  $day  = substr( $datetime, 6, 2 );
  $hour = substr( $datetime, 8, 2 );
  $min  = substr( $datetime, 10, 2 );
  $sec  = substr( $datetime, 12, 2 );
  $orgdate = date("l F dS, Y h:i A",
      mktime( $hour, $min, $sec, $mon, $day, $year ) );
  echo( "Time of entry: " . $orgdate ); }
?>
</body></html>
```

This example splits the timestamp into separate components. These are made into a time object with the mktime() function, then formatted for display by the date() function – see page 64 for more on date formatting.

The same routine is used in the script on the next page, which displays entries from the guestbook database table.

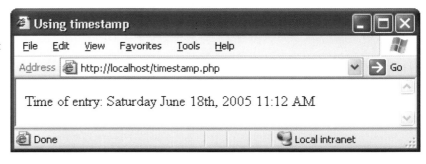

Time of entry: Saturday June 18th, 2005 11:12 AM

Viewing the guestbook

Following the link on page 170 loads the guestbook-view.php script listed below. This extracts the data from each field of the latest three records in the guestbook database table, arranged in descending time order.

The script writes a HTML table for each record and displays the stored name, email address, comments and formatted entry time.

guestbook-view.php

The SQL query in this example will extract data from only the latest three entries because the SQL limit specifies a value of 3.

```php
<html><head><title>View guestbook</title></head>
<body><h3>Latest 3 guestbook entries...</h3>

<?php
  $rs = @mysql_connect( "localhost", "mike", "bingo" );
  $rs = @mysql_select_db( "my_database" );

  #SQL query for last 3 entries in descending time order
  $sql =
   "select * from guestbook order by time desc limit 3";
  $rs = @mysql_query( $sql );

  #loop through records writing a table for each one
  while ( $row = mysql_fetch_array( $rs ) )
  {
?>
  <table border="1" width="375">
  <tr>
  <td><b>Name:</b> <?php echo $row["name"]; ?></td>
  <td><b>Email:</b>
  <a href="mailto:<?php echo $row["email"]; ?>">
  <?php echo $row["email"]; ?></a> </td></tr>
  <tr><td colspan="2">

<?php $datetime = $row["time"];
      $year = substr( $datetime, 0, 4 );
      $mon  = substr( $datetime, 4, 2 );
      $day  = substr( $datetime, 6, 2 );
      $hour = substr( $datetime, 8, 2 );
      $min  = substr( $datetime, 10, 2 );
      $sec  = substr( $datetime, 12, 2 );
      $orgdate = date("l F dS, Y h:i A",
      mktime( $hour, $min, $sec, $mon, $day, $year ) );
?>
```

guestbook-view.php
(continued)

```
Date: <?php echo $orgdate; ?></td></tr>
<tr><td colspan="2"><b>Comments:</b>
<?php echo $row["comments"]; ?></td></tr>
</table>
<br>

<?php } ?>

</body></html>
```

Even with ten entries added to the guestbook database table, the script generates HTML tables for only the last three entries. The visitor's email address is formatted as a link with the "mailto:" protocol to make email response simpler.

Clicking a hyperlink that uses the mailto: protocol will open your default email client application with the target address already completed – just type a reply then send the email response.

Saving the guestbook

The mysqldump program, located in MySQL's bin directory, can be used to save any MySQL database or table as a text file.

To save the guestbook table created in this chapter, first navigate from a command prompt to MySQL's bin directory. Type "mysqldump --help" to see a list of options. The common syntax to save a single table is:

mysqldump [*options* **]** *database-name table-name* **>** *file-name*

Use a "-t" option (to suppress the table creation info) followed by the "my_database" name and "guestbook" table name. Finally, use the ">" character to direct output to a file named "guestbook.txt".

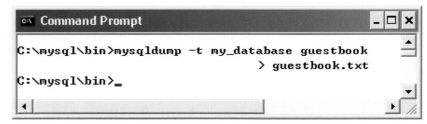

The text file gets created in the bin directory unless a path precedes the filename, such as > C:\guestbook.txt.

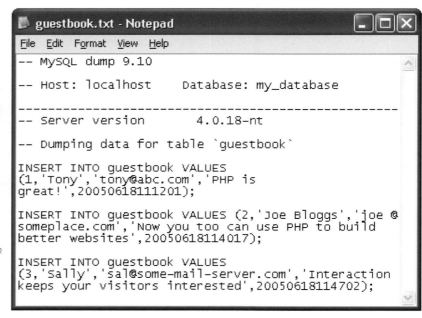

PHP and XML

This chapter demonstrates how PHP can be used with XML documents. It shows how to selectively extract data from them for output to a web browser, and how PHP scripts can add data to an XML document.

Covers

Chapter Fourteen

Introducing XML

PHP version 5 introduces enhanced support for object oriented programming and completely new support features for the increasingly important XML (eXtensible Markup Language). Its XML support is now compliant with the W3C (World Wide Web Consortium) specifications – unlike that in previous releases.

PHP 5 supports DOM (Document Object Model) according to the W3C standard, and the XPath query language. It also incorporates the PHP-specific "SimpleXML" extension. Examples of DOM, XPath and SimpleXML are given in this chapter.

XML is a popular means of storing data, which adopts a very strict syntax. It looks very much like HTML, complete with tags, attributes, and values, but XML has no predefined tags and it is not used to create web pages directly. Instead, XML lets you create your own custom markup tags and define how these tags may be used.

Comprehensive descriptions and demonstrations of the power of XML are available in "XML in easy steps".

In XML each opening tag must have a matching closing tag, and tag pairs must be correctly nested. XML documents that meet these syntax requirements are said to be "well-formed". The great advantage for applications handling well-formed XML data is that they need not allow for incorrect syntax – unlike web browsers handling HTML documents, which include a lot of tolerance code.

All XML documents begin with a declaration tag, which announces that the document is using XML. This typically includes attributes that describe the version and character encoding type, like this:

```
<?xml version = "1.0" encoding = "iso-8859-1" ?>
```

Here the declaration specifies that this document is written with XML version 1.0 in the common Latin character set.

All XML documents must have a main tag element that encloses all other tags. This tag is more correctly called the "root" element.

```
<?xml version = "1.0" encoding = "iso-8859-1" ?>

<root>

  <greeting>Hello World</greeting>

</root>
```

hello.xml

In the well-formed XML document hello.xml, listed opposite, the root element is actually named "root". The nested element named "greeting" contains text content of "Hello World".

In practice most XML documents contain many tags, describing a great deal of data. For instance, the books.xml document, listed below, contains data describing some other books in this series. Within the "books" root element each "title" element contains nested tags for "topic", the "series" name, and the name of an image file of that book's cover within an element called "pic".

books.xml

Opening a XML document in a web browser, such as Internet Explorer, displays the XML tags in "tree" format if the document is well-formed. Otherwise, an error message indicates the cause of the error.

```xml
<?xml version = "1.0" encoding = "iso-8859-1" ?>

<books>

  <title>
     <topic>JavaScript</topic>
     <series>in easy steps</series>
     <pic>js.gif</pic>
  </title>

  <title>
     <topic>C++ Programming</topic>
     <series>in easy steps</series>
     <pic>c++.gif</pic>
  </title>

  <title>
     <topic>HTML</topic>
     <series>in easy steps</series>
     <pic>html.gif</pic>
  </title>

  <title>
     <topic>SQL</topic>
     <series>in easy steps</series>
     <pic>sql.gif</pic>
  </title>

</books>
```

This XML document is used by some examples in this chapter to demonstrate XML support features in PHP 5.

Reading from the DOM

PHP 5 has built-in support for the Document Object Model (DOM) as specified by the W3C standard. This provides a "DomDocument" template class containing predefined variables and methods (or **functions**).

A DomDocument object can be created in a PHP script by using the "new" keyword to assign an instance of the class to a variable. For example, $dom = new DomDocument creates a DomDocument object in the $dom variable.

The variable properties and the methods of an object can be referenced using the special class pointer operator "->". For instance, the DomDocument object has a load() method to load an XML file, so that $dom -> load("books.xml") loads the data from the file "books.xml" into the $dom object.

Each element of the XML document is described as a "node".

The root element of the XML document can be addressed using the DomDocument object's "documentElement" property, and its tag name can be referenced from its inherent "nodeName" part. For example, $dom -> documentElement -> nodeName.

The textContent property is not an actual W3C standard – it is a PHP convenience property, used to access all text nodes of an element quickly.

Specific nested elements of the XML document can be addressed using the DomDocument object's "getElementsByTagName()" method, which takes the name of the required element as its parameter. This method returns a "DomNodeList", which a script can easily loop through using the foreach() function. The textual data of each node can be referenced by the "textContent" property, which PHP provides.

The script opposite first creates a DomDocument object, then loads the "books.xml" document (listed on the previous page). It proceeds to generate HTML output stating the XML document's root element name and a list of all the text data contained within its "topic" elements.

...cont'd

read-dom.php

```
<html><head><title>Read DOM</title></head><body>

<?php

#load an xml document into the DOM
$dom = new DomDocument;
$dom -> load( "books.xml" );

#print out the root element name
echo( "Root element name is: " );
echo( $dom -> documentElement -> nodeName );
echo( "<hr>" );

#print a list of all topics
echo( "Topics include:<ul>" );
$topics = $dom -> getElementsByTagName( "topic" );
foreach( $topics as $node )
{
  echo( "<li>" . $node -> textContent . "</li>" );
}
echo( "</ul>" );

?>

</body></html>
```

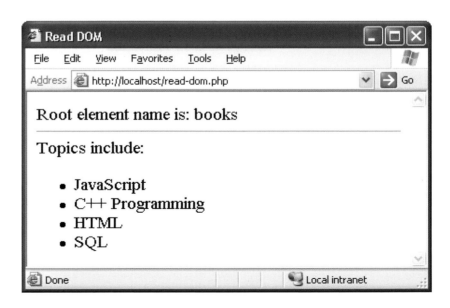

Writing to the DOM

The DomDocument object includes methods to manipulate and write to the DOM. New elements can be created with the createElement() method and text content can be inserted with the createTextNode() method. Each text node is added to its surrounding element, and each element added to its higher-level element, with the appendChild() method.

This example adds a complete new book to those in books.xml and creates a new, enlarged XML document using the save() method.

write-dom.php

```php
<?php

$dom = new DomDocument();
$dom -> load( "books.xml" );

#create elements
$title =  $dom -> createElement( "title" );
$topic =  $dom -> createElement( "topic" );
$series = $dom -> createElement( "series" );
$pic =    $dom -> createElement( "pic" );

#create text nodes
$topictext =  $dom -> createTextNode( "Linux" );
$seriestext = $dom -> createTextNode( "in easy steps" );
$pictext =    $dom -> createTextNode( "linux.gif" );

#append the text nodes to the inner nested elements
$topic  -> appendChild( $topictext );
$series -> appendChild( $seriestext );
$pic    -> appendChild( $pictext );

#append the inner nested elements to the <title> element
$title -> appendChild( $topic );
$title -> appendChild( $series );
$title -> appendChild( $pic );

#now append the <title> element to the root element
$dom -> documentElement -> appendChild( $title );

#create a new enlarged XML document
$dom -> save( "newbooks.xml" );

?>
```

Opening the new XML document in a web browser confirms that each new element has been correctly added, nested inside the root element. They appear after the final original "title" element, with the appropriate specified text content inserted as expected.

Although this example saves the changes in a new document, the DOM can be manipulated "on the fly" and new elements accessed dynamically.

Querying with XPath

XPath allows you to query an XML document for specific nodes matching particular criteria. This is far more powerful than the getElementsByTagName() method, which simply returns a DomNodeList of all elements having the specified name. For instance, given the XML document food.xml (listed below), a call to getElementsByTagName("item") would return all the "item" child elements of both "fruit" and "veg" elements.

food.xml

```
<?xml version = "1.0" encoding = "iso-8859-1" ?>

<food>

  <fruit>
    <item id = "1">Apple</item>
    <item id = "2">Banana</item>
    <item id = "3">Cherry</item>
  </fruit>

  <veg>
    <item>Lettuce</item>
    <item>Onion</item>
  </veg>

</food>
```

XPath, however, can return specific elements.

To start using XPath in PHP 5, a DomXPath object must first be created using the "new" keyword and stating the name of the loaded DomDocument as its parameter. The DomXPath object is assigned to a variable in the same manner as with a new DomDocument object.

The query path begins with a "/" character.

Significantly, the DomXPath object has a query() method that returns a DomNodeList of those nodes matching the criteria specified as its parameter. The simplest query specifies the path to a particular element, such as "/food/fruit/item".

The PHP script listed opposite assigns a DomXPath object to a variable called "$xp". Its query() method is used to return a DomNodeList of all "item" nodes within the "fruit" element. Their textContent data is then written out in a HTML list.

xpath-query.php

```
<html><head><title>XPath DOM Query</title></head><body>

<?php        #load the XML document into the DOM
             $dom = new DomDocument();
             $dom -> load( "food.xml" );

             #create an XPath object
             $xp = new DomXPath( $dom );

#print a list of all fruit items
echo( "Fruit items are:<ul>" );
$fruits = $xp -> query( "/food/fruit/item" );
foreach( $fruits as $node )
{  echo( "<li>" . $node -> textContent . "</li>" ); }
echo( "</ul>" );
?>
</body></html>
```

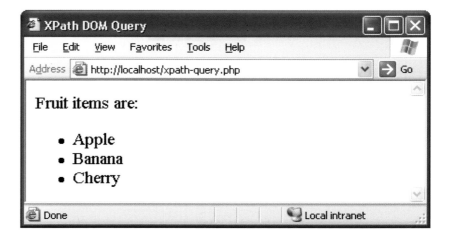

This is just a simple example. Further query possibilities might be:

- query("/food/fruit/item[position() = 1]") – returns just the first "item" element nested within the "fruit" element.

- query("/food/fruit/item[@id='2']") – returns just the "item" element having an "id" attribute value of "2".

- query("/food/veg/item") – returns all the "item" elements nested within the "veg" element.

Using SimpleXML

PHP version 5 includes the "SimpleXML" extension. The goal of SimpleXML is to provide easy access to XML documents using standard object properties.

The simplexml_load_file() function takes the name of an XML document, loads it into a SimpleXML object, and returns it. As usual, the foreach() function can loop through the nodes to access a specific element, but now their nested elements are easily referenced using the "->" pointer operator.

The script below loops through each "title" element of the books.xml document listed on page 177. It references each element nested within those "title" elements using the "->" pointer operator, and generates a HTML table of the XML data.

simple-xml.php

```php
<html><head><title>SimpleXML</title></head><body>

<?php

#load an XML document into a SimpleXML object
$sx = simplexml_load_file( "books.xml" );

#create a table of books data
print "<table width = '375px' cellpadding = '5px'
                border = '1px' cellspacing = '0px'>";

foreach( $sx -> title as $title )
{
  echo( "<tr>" );
  echo( "<td align = 'right'>" );
  echo( "<img src = '" . $title -> pic . "'>" );
  echo( "</td>" );
  echo( "<td valign = 'top'>" );
  echo( "<b>"  . $title -> topic . "</b>" );
  echo( "<br>" . $title -> series );
  echo( "</td>" );
  echo( "</tr>" );
}
echo( "</table>" );
?>

</body></html>
```

The full line of titles in this series can be explored in good book stores and online at www.ineasysteps.com.

The DOM and SimpleXML provide complementary tools for processing XML document data in PHP scripts. Conveniently, SimpleXML objects can be easily converted to DomDocument objects, and vice versa. This lets you use the tool best suited for the job in hand. The conversion functions look like this:

- $dom = dom_import_simplexml($sx) – converts a SimpleXML object to a DomDocument object

- $sx = simplexml_import_dom($dom) – converts a DomDocument object to a SimpleXML object

The examples in this chapter utilize the most popular functions to process XML data. Details of other SimpleXML and DOM functions are provided in the PHP documentation, available online at www.php.net.

More PHP resources

This book will, hopefully, have provided you with a great introduction to PHP server-side scripting, and may have inspired you with some of PHP's creative possibilities.

The many PHP functions used in the examples throughout this book are, in fact, just a small selection from the hundreds of functions that are available in the PHP scripting language. To see the entire range of functions, and to go further with PHP, it is recommended that you now download the PHP manual from www.php.net/download-docs.php.

The manual is available in several languages and many formats, including HTML, PDF and Windows HLP format. It is very comprehensive and has a section called Function Reference, which defines each function on its own page. These are grouped under topic headings and many contain examples illustrating how they can be used in a PHP script.

The PHP Builder website at www.phpbuilder.com is a terrific resource offering interesting articles about PHP. This site also has several forums where help can be sought on PHP scripting. Some source code is available for free download and you can even access the PHP manual online there.

Another great online resource is the PHP Resource Index website at http://php.resourceindex.com. This site has lots of useful code snippets and offers hundreds of complete PHP scripts – although not all of these are available free.

The site's Documentation section contains examples and tutorials with lots of handy tips. The Frequently Asked Questions (FAQ) pages can be scoured for previous answers to PHP questions.

In the Community section there are links to many PHP-related bulletin boards on the Internet where you can find other PHP developers. There is information about PHP mailing lists, development tools, user groups and lots more.

The huge popularity of PHP, as a scripting language especially suited to web development, ensures its continuing success – happy scripting with PHP!

Index

! logical not   34
!= inequality operator   38
single-line comment   21
% modulus operator   32
&& logical and   34
* multiply   32
+ add   32
++ increment   32
- subtract   32
-- decrement   32
. concatenate strings   32
/ divide   32
/* ... */ multi-line comment   21
// single-line comment   21
< less than operator   38
= assignment operator   36
== equality operator   36
> greater than operator   38
|| logical or   34
\ backslash character   22
\n newline   22, 89, 118
\r carriage return   118
\t tab character   22

access limitation cookie   102
addition   32
advantages of PHP   9
alter table (SQL command)   135, 151
and keyword   23
Apache
   configuration   16
   installation   12
   starting & stopping   13
appendChild() method   180
appending data   89
array elements   52
array keyword   23
array size   55
array() function   52
array_merge() function   60

array_pop() function   57
array_push() function   56
array_shift() function   57
array_slice() function   60
array_unshift() function   56
as keyword   23, 54
assign data   24
assignment operators   36
attachment form   120
authenticated log-in   164
authorised users   158

B

backslash character \   22
base64_encode() function   122
boolean data type   25
break keyword   23, 44, 48
browse button   120
browser re-direction   76

C

cache control   74
carriage return \r   118
case keyword   23, 44
case-sensitive   21
cfunction keyword   23
chunk_split() function   122
class keyword   23
class pointer operator ->   178
closedir() function   80
column   128
comments   21
conditional branching   44
const keyword   23

M

N

O

P

T

U